1. Introduction

In 1970, the Carnegie Commission on Higher Education and the Ford Foundation jointly sponsored a study of the financial conditions of colleges and universities. They did so in response to the request of several college and university presidents who were concerned about the downward direction of their own campuses' fiscal situation and saw increasing reason for alarm when the current trends were projected into the future. The study sought to determine how general the financial problem was and what institutions of various types were doing in response to it. The study included institutions from each of six major categories: national research universities, leading regional research universities, state and comprehensive colleges, liberal arts colleges, primarily black colleges, and two-year colleges. In all, the study examined the financial condition of 41 colleges and universities. The data were gathered in May, June, and early July of 1970.

The results of the study were published in March 1971 in a Carnegie Commission general report, *The New Depression in Higher Education.*[1] The principal finding was that the difficult experiences of the concerned presidents were not isolated fiscal events, but were part of a general erosion of the financial position of most colleges and universities. Expenditures were rising faster than income and the resulting gap was putting most of America's colleges and universities under heavy and increasing financial pressures. Not all institutions were affected equally, but all were affected to some degree.

The effect on institutions that the study was concerned with was that of financial condition on academic program and quality. Institutions whose financial condition forced a reduction in neither academic services nor quality were judged to be "not in financial trouble." The others were classified as "in financial difficulty" or "headed for

---

[1] This report was published as part of the Carnegie Commission's series. Copies are available from the McGraw-Hill Book Company, 1221 Avenue of the Americas, New York.

trouble," depending on whether they were judged to have already made reductions in their academic services or quality or were certain to be forced to do so in the near future. Of the 41 institutions in the study, 12 (29 percent) were found to be not in financial trouble at the time of the campus visit. The remaining 29 (71 percent) were judged headed for financial trouble or already in difficulty. Using the data and criteria from the study, the Carnegie Commission staff estimated that about three-fifths of the nation's colleges and universities were in trouble or headed for it. The essence of the problem was an increasingly serious cost-income gap: Income growth was declining but the rate of growth of expenditures was steady or even increasing.

Two other studies conducted in 1970—one by William W. Jellema (1971) of the Association of American Colleges and the other by Hans H. Jenny and G. Richard Wynn (1970) of the College of Wooster—produced additional evidence that this gap between expenditure and income was not the kind of economic problem traditionally faced by colleges and universities. Academic institutions have always faced the problem generated in labor-intensive enterprises—in which costs rise faster than productivity. The traditional (and necessary) response to that problem has been to seek increased income. Now, *The New Depression* and the other studies were finding something new: First, the cost problem could in significant part be attributed to unusual growth in the academic responsibilities, activities, and aspirations of colleges and universities; second, the cost problem was aggravated by a high rate of inflation; and, third, there was a reduced rate of income growth due to increased competition for funds, changed attitudes toward higher education, and a growing gap between the tuition charged at public and private institutions.

For higher education, these factors were bringing to an end what Jenny's study called the "Golden Years" and were creating what I called "The New Depression." Whatever one called it, by 1971 the fact had become clear: For most colleges and universities, expenditures were growing faster than income, and projections of the future size of the resulting gap indicated that campuses would be beset by hard times.

In the two years since publication of *The New Depression in Higher Education*, the money problems of higher education have grown to become its dominant concern. College and university presidents consistently report that their major problem is the choices forced on them by the cost-income situation on campus. The conversations at meetings of various associations in higher education reveal the same situation. Whether it is the Association of University Presses, or the National Collegiate Athletic Association, or the learned societies, or the land-grant colleges, the conversations are never far from the money problem on campus and its consequences for the students, the institutions, and the society at large.

The New Depression in Higher Education— Two Years Later

by Earl F. Cheit

Professor of Business Administration
University of California, Berkeley
(on leave as Program Officer,
Division of Higher Education and Research,
The Ford Foundation, New York)

A Technical Report Sponsored by
The Carnegie Commission on Higher Education

The Carnegie Commission on Higher Education,
1947 Center Street, Berkeley, California 94704,
has sponsored preparation of this report as a
part of a continuing effort to obtain and present
significant information for public discussion.
The views expressed are those of the authors.

THE NEW DEPRESSION IN HIGHER EDUCATION—
TWO YEARS LATER

Library of Congress catalog card number 73-80150.

Contents

iii

Acknowledgments

I would like to thank the administrators at each of the 41 colleges and universities who helped us by providing information for this follow-up study. Although the demands of our questionnaire were relatively modest, they came at a time when the total number of such requests for information is becoming burdensome to colleges and universities. I am grateful to these administrators for this generous cooperation.

Karl W. Payne, Esq., worked on the questionnaire, reestablished contact with many of the campus administrators, and analyzed the expenditure data. Mrs. Barbara Porter typed the manuscript. Mrs. Dorris Fennell helped gather some of the stray data and typed an early draft.

My Colleague, Robert H. Cole, professor of law and student of higher education, read the entire manuscript and made many contributions to the final draft. I want to acknowledge my debt to him.

Finally, I want to thank the Carnegie Commission and the Ford Foundation for their help and to exempt both from responsibility for any interpretations or views I have expressed.

Earl F. Cheit

Westport, Conn.
March 1973

Foreword

The New Depression in Higher Education was a landmark book when it appeared in 1971. It had several immediate impacts: (1) colleges could now talk about their individual situations openly—financial trouble was no longer a "social disease" not open to public discussion, one that had to be suffered in solitude; (2) the federal government and many states became more interested in the financial welfare of institutions of higher education, both public and private; and (3) colleges, and their component parts, began concentrating on cost reduction as well as on income augmentation.

Now Earl Cheit has taken a look at the same institutions two years later. His major finding is that now, after their past descent from the "golden years," they have generally reached a plateau of "fragile stability." But in 1973 as in 1971 the situation is marked by great diversity. No single pattern exists; in fact, no two institutions are exactly alike in how they have been affected and how they have responded. Broadly speaking, however, private institutions seem to have adjusted more quickly and more adequately than public institutions, and research universities have been affected most adversely of all—yet they, in particular, are most widely related to the national welfare.

The reduction of the rate of increase of costs has been almost phenomenal. In terms of rising expenditure per student per year above the general rate of inflation, the rate of increase for this group of institutions has gone down from nearly 4.0 percent in the earlier period to 0.5 percent. This corresponds with the long-term rate of 2.5 percent, which is also the rate for the future recommended by the Carnegie Commission as being one at which quality can be maintained. The 0.5 percent rate cannot be sustained indefinitely without loss of quality. Some recent cost reductions are of the once-and-for-all type, such as dropping a department or school. Others can be sustained better in the short-run than in the long-run, without loss of quality. Among them is raising the student-faculty ratio, which has been one major way of holding down costs. Nevertheless, a number of institutions have thus far made cost adjustments both quickly and effectively, and with minimum or even no loss of quality. The record is a most impressive one.

Two particularly interesting developments are: (1) the more central role accorded to administration in the new environment; and (2) the securing of change by the process of substitution rather than through growth—and this is a very tough way to get change.

The future is uncertain. What will be the course of public and private support to institutions? How much external support will there be for student aid—an area of cost most troublesome to many institutions? What will happen to enrollments? How much general inflation will there be?

In the interim, however, the institutions in this study have made heroic efforts to control their costs. They have clearly demonstrated that they can make better use of their resources, albeit that this demonstration has been made under duress. They should, in the course of all of this, be building renewed public confidence in the quality of their administrations.

Clark Kerr
Chairman, Carnegie Commission
on Higher Education

March 1973

That situation was summarized by Ernest Boyer, president of the State University of New York, who observed in a speech to a national gathering of administrators considering ways of dealing with financial problems, that throughout the 1970s, "higher education will be expected to do more with less" (*Chronicle*, 1972, p. 4).

To do more (or even as much) with less requires changes on the campus, and even at this early stage of the "new depression" the changes have become important. Most obvious of these is a growing cost-consciousness on campus. If it could ever be said of the leaders in higher education that they know the value of everything but the cost of nothing, no one could make that accusation today. Today we are more likely to hear the worry of a pressed faculty union that those in charge know the cost of everything but the value of nothing.

The financial problems of higher education have done more than stimulate cost-consciousness. They have led to significant new policies and practices on the campuses. In addition, the question of how to finance higher education has engaged the interest of a growing number of economists. It has produced a major management movement, complete with new techniques and a new vocabulary, and it has stimulated policy reviews by important organizations like the Committee for Economic Development. It has produced influential state studies in Washington, New York, and many states between. It has stimulated the invention of new devices for increasing income—the Common Fund (for cooperation in managing endowments) is one example; the income-contingent loan (deferred tuition) is another. It has brought action in about one-third of the states to increase public support of the private sector, and for some months, it commanded the attention of the Congress of the United States.

Once the issues became clear, the Congress acted with remarkable speed in trying to respond to the fiscal problems of higher education. Although there were some preliminary hearings in 1969, serious legislative action did not begin until late 1971. By then, in addition to various studies of the problem, there had been sharp increases in deficits, in tuition, and in anxieties. As reports of financial stress came in from individual campuses and various agencies concerned with higher education, Congressional recognition that this was a serious problem came quickly. The legislative response, the Higher Education Amendments of 1972, was adopted in May.

Thus, the new financial problem that had been the private concern of a few college and university presidents was, within just three years, to become the major premise in a national effort to develop new policies for higher education.

2. The Hope for a Federal Solution and What Came of It

As Congress worked to develop new public policy toward higher education, the college presidents' perspective did not remain the guiding viewpoint for very long. Their institutional view of the financial problem was soon paired with a second perspective of the new financial problem of higher education—that of the low-income student. Two approaches—institutional aid and student aid—became the focal points in a legislative struggle of considerable symbolic significance. Much oversimplified, one approach sought to provide financial assistance directly to institutions and to deal separately with student aid. It was opposed by those who thought the institutional aid formula was an indiscriminate approach, and by those who thought the student aid commitment inadequate to deal with the needs of the poor and minorities. The other approach sought to provide aid to low-income students and grants to those institutions enrolling low-income students. It was opposed by those who found it inadequately tailored to institutional needs and also by those who felt that it ignored the fast-growing needs of middle-income students.

The highly complicated legislative compromise that resulted comes closer to the student-aid approach. The 1972 amendments, among other things, provide "basic opportunity grants" to needy students, with additional cost-of-education allowances to institutions payable only when student grants under the 1972 and earlier acts have been funded at specified levels.

Even among those disappointed by the legislation, hopes were high last spring, for Congress had enacted important programs and authorized substantial sums to students and to institutions. But by now these hopes have been dimmed, first by the failure of the government to commit funds to implement the legislation, and more recently by growing uncertainty about whether these new programs will ever have real meaning. Congressional commitment to the 1972 act has at best been tentative, and administration commitment has at best been selective. The combined effect has been delay, arguments over technical requirements, and general uncertainty. The most optimistic predictions are that there will be some kind of "basic opportunity grant" program in operation by next fall (academic year 1973-74).

The earnest hope that the federal government was going to make a dramatic legislative move that would in large measure relieve the financial pressure on the nation's colleges and universities ended in disappointment, recriminations, and calls for reorganizing the lobbying efforts of the higher education associations.

Although the Higher Education Amendments did not constitute a coherent federal strategy toward higher education, they did produce the basic-opportunity grant program, and with it, the possibility of significant, new federal commitment to extension of access to higher education. That important result depends on funding, and as of now, that part of the act has had no effect on institutions in this study. Moreover, most of the administrators in these colleges and universities do not believe it is likely to have much effect on their institutions in the very near future.

In addition to a promise to extend opportunities for access, the federal response to the financial problems of higher education had another product: It confirmed that for institutions of higher education to obtain substantial federal help today it is not enough just to be in need. That point was already understood by many of the administrators interviewed in the original *New Depression* study. In that study we concluded (pp. 154-156) that substantial new investment in higher education would require, in addition to need, that three conditions be met: First, that the college and university campuses reveal themselves as being reasonably governable; second, that the colleges and universities demonstrate that they are reasonably efficient in their internal operations; and finally, that there be evidence that the activities of colleges and universities have a unifying set of purposes—purposes that the public can understand and support.

The first condition—that campuses reveal themselves as reasonably governable—appears to have been met. But concern about the other two conditions has increased substantially in the two years since the original study. There is a persistent public concern that these expensive and hard-to-understand enterprises—the colleges and universities—are not as cost-effective as they should be. And there is a sizable, although not well-focused, dissatisfaction about the purposes and values of higher education. If one accepts the hypothesis that not just institutional financial need but also effective satisfaction of these other conditions is prerequisite to substantial new investment in higher education, then it is not surprising that Congress would postpone appropriations and rely instead on an essentially procedural response to the new depression.

Whether for that reason or others, that is precisely what Congress has done. We have already noted its failure to appropriate funds; let us now look at its procedural responses.

Three procedural elements in the Higher Education Amendments are especially noteworthy. First of these is the provision for state commissions. Under section 1202 of the legislation, each state is authorized to establish a commission for the purposes of planning for postsecondary and occupational education in the state. Since the establishment of such commissions is made a requirement for the states to receive certain categories of federal assistance, there is ample incentive for each state to establish a section 1202 commission. There are technical problems in some states—statutory changes, for example—but most important is the overall fact that all forms of postsecondary education, including proprietary, would now be included in a state planning process required by the federal government.[1]

A second procedural response is a major, national study called for by section 140(a)(1) of the statute. The charge to the National Commission on the Financing of Postsecondary Education created by the act explicitly reflects the view that differences about approach to the financial problem have not been resolved in Congress. It states ". . . such study shall determine the need, the desirability, the form, and the level of additional governmental and private assistance." The commission is getting its study under way in early 1973, and it hopes to have its findings and recommendations available early in the congressional session of 1974. The commission is asked to provide national uniform standard procedures for determining the annual per-student costs of providing postsecondary education for students attending various types of educational institutions. These are to be included in the legislative recommendations to be made by the Commissioner of Education following the study.

Finally, the approach being followed in the limited implementation of the act in the proposed federal budget suggests that there is a strong federal disposition to encourage "market forces" to operate; funds would be given not to institutions, but to students, and the market process will begin to define the values of education.

Together, therefore, these procedural elements suggest that the failure to make the new higher education legislation effective in its substantive parts is not just a case of uncertainty about what to do in response to the needs of higher education. What has been set in motion is an effort to redefine these needs through: The planning required at

---

[1] Even the 1202 commissions have a financial problem. Acting Education Commissioner John Ottina announced on March 9 that activity on these commissions was being suspended because, "The federal budget for fiscal year 1974 provides almost no functions for the section 1202 state commissions to perform" (Ottina, 1973, p. 1).

the state level; the work of the study commission; the development of uniform standards for cost data; and eventually through the "market power" of student choice.

The effects of this evolving federal situation, along with the growing centralization of governance of higher education within the states, cannot yet be discerned, of course, in the financial condition of the 41 schools whose 1970 experience was reported in the *New Depression*. But the effects will be significant and, as we shall see, are likely to reinforce some tendencies that are discernible in this restudy of the 41 campuses.

Back on the campuses, life goes on. The passage of two years affords some opportunity to confirm or revise observations in the original study and to determine whether the situation of the colleges and universities has changed. Hence, the present study is a modest return check on the 41 institutions in the 1971 study. The general conclusion we draw is that the schools' financial deterioration has been slowed and, in fact, a certain degree of stability, fragile but real, has been achieved.

3. The New Depression—Two Years Later

THE FOLLOW-UP
STUDY Beginning in spring, 1972, and through the summer months, administrators (usually the president or the chancellor) at each of the 41 colleges and universities in *The New Depression in Higher Education* were asked to participate in a follow-up study. At each institution, administrators indicated their willingness to participate. Each was then sent the questionnaire included as an appendix to this report, and all 41 returned them by late fall, 1972. The data thus obtained, on which the present study is based, were gathered almost exactly two years after the data on which *New Depression* was based. Unlike the earlier study, this follow-up did not include visits to the campuses, and the questionnaire was less detailed. It sought administrators' assessments of the financial situation, information about the campus' response to its financial situation, and expenditure data for each year since 1969-70. It did not ask for income data.[1]

Listed alphabetically the 41 institutions included in the original and this follow-up study are as follows:

Albion College, Albion, Michigan
Allegheny College, Meadville, Pennsylvania
Beloit College, Beloit, Wisconsin
Boston College, Chestnut Hill, Massachusetts
Carleton College, Northfield, Minnesota
Central Michigan University, Mount Pleasant, Michigan
City Colleges of Chicago, Chicago, Illinois

---

[1] Partly this was a decision to avoid an undue burden on the 41 institutions; partly it was due to the realization that without a detailed analysis of the accounts of individual institutions, it is difficult to evaluate simple statements of income, or reports of deficits. In the original study, one institution reported an income shortfall, which we reported. It later appeared that the deficit was not an operating deficit but the result of a transfer of funds to capital accounts. Some income information was reported by individual institutions in the follow-up study. It appears at appropriate places in the text.

College of San Mateo, San Mateo, California
Cumberland College, Williamsberg, Kentucky
Fisk University, Nashville, Tennessee
Flint Community Junior College, Flint, Michigan*
Gulf Coast Junior College, Panama City, Florida
Hamilton College, Clinton, New York
Harvard University, Cambridge, Massachusetts
Howard University, Washington, D.C.
Huston-Tillotson College, Austin, Texas
Knox College, Galesburg, Illinois
Meredith College, Raleigh, North Carolina
Mesa College, Grand Junction, Colorado
Mills College, Oakland, California
Morgan State College, Baltimore, Maryland
New York University, New York, New York
Ohio University, Athens, Ohio
Pomona College, Claremont, California
Portland State University, Portland, Oregon
Saint Cloud State College, St. Cloud, Minnesota
Saint Louis University, St. Louis, Missouri
San Diego State College, San Diego, California†
Stanford University, Stanford, California
Syracuse University, Syracuse, New York
Tougaloo College, Tougaloo, Mississippi
Tulane University, New Orleans, Louisiana
University of California, Berkeley, California
University of Chicago, Chicago, Illinois
University of Michigan, Ann Arbor, Michigan
University of Minnesota, Minneapolis, Minnesota
University of Missouri, Columbia, Missouri
University of North Carolina, Chapel Hill, North Carolina
University of Oregon, Eugene, Oregon
University of Texas, Austin, Texas
Whitman College, Walla Walla, Washington

*Renamed Genessee Community College since the original study. For convenience in cross-referencing to the original study, we will retain the original name here.

†Renamed California State University at San Diego. For convenience in cross-referencing, we will retain the original name here.

The sample comprises a reasonably illustrative mix of institutions within each of six major types:

National Research Universities
Harvard University
Stanford University
University of California, Berkeley
University of Chicago
University of Michigan
University of Minnesota, Minneapolis
University of Texas, Austin

Leading Regional Research Universities
New York University
Ohio University
Saint Louis University
Syracuse University
Tulane University
University of Missouri, Columbia
University of North Carolina, Chapel Hill
University of Oregon

State and Comprehensive Colleges
Boston College
Central Michigan University
Portland State University
Saint Cloud State College
San Diego State College

Liberal Arts Colleges
Albion College
Allegheny College
Beloit College
Carleton College
Cumberland College
Hamilton College
Knox College
Meredith College
Mills College
Pomona College
Whitman College

Primarily Black Colleges
Fisk University
Howard University
Huston-Tillotson College
Morgan State College
Tougaloo College

Two-Year Colleges
City Colleges of Chicago
College of San Mateo
Flint Community Junior College
Gulf Coast Junior College
Mesa College

Twenty-three of these schools are private institutions, eighteen are public. They are listed here with their 1968[2] and their 1971 opening fall enrollments as reported to the original *New Depression* study and this follow-up.

---

[2]This, the following two paragraphs, and the map are reprinted from *The New Depression in Higher Education* (1971).

TABLE 1   Opening fall enrollments 1968 and 1971

Private	Fall 1968	Fall 1971
Albion College	1,801	1,809
Allegheny College	1,595	1,725
Beloit College	1,761	1,742
Boston College	9,972	11,111
Carleton College	1,451	1,490
Cumberland College	1,771	1,769
Fisk University	1,161	1,414
Hamilton College	853	940
Harvard University	15,198	15,401
Howard University	8,704	9,456
Huston-Tillotson College	832	655
Knox College	1,371	1,437
Meredith College	859	1,291
Mills College	792	974
New York University	33,562	35,400
Pomona College	1,313	1,303
Saint Louis University	9,768	10,490
Stanford University	12,045	11,626
Syracuse University	17,864	21,550*
Tougaloo College	714	752
Tulane University	8,359	8,732
University of Chicago	8,286	7,610
Whitman College	1,103	1,072

*Includes Utica College.

As the map indicates, the 41 institutions are located in 21 states and the District of Columbia. Fourteen of the schools are in the Midwest, ten in the West, nine in the South, and eight in the East.

This sample of 41 institutions was not designed to be statistically representative of all American institutions of higher education. Nor is there any special significance in the number "41." That number resulted from an effort to include several examples of all major types of institutions and at the same time to keep the size of the sample within manageable limits. The schools selected were ones whose experience we thought would be *illustrative* of the major types of colleges and universities. No attempt was made to select any institution because of its financial situation, favorable or unfavorable. Financial situation was not considered in selecting the 41 schools.

Public	Fall 1968	Fall 1971
Central Michigan University	13,419	14,913
City Colleges of Chicago, 8 campuses	30,208	46,833
College of San Mateo	10,677	13,190
Flint Community Junior College	7,091	11,951
Gulf Coast Junior College	1,807	1,640
Mesa College	2,889	3,210
Morgan State College	4,391	5,743
Ohio University	22,067	23,914
Portland State University	10,206	13,601
Saint Cloud State College	9,267	10,061
San Diego State College	30,077	32,149
University of California, Berkeley	28,132	27,712
University of Michigan	38,021	39,986
University of Minnesota, Minneapolis	46,881	51,245
University of Missouri, Columbia	20,953	21,942
University of North Carolina, Chapel Hill	16,233	20,882
University of Oregon	14,761	15,249
University of Texas, Austin	33,797	39,503

Two additional introductory observations should be made about the findings drawn in this study from the follow-up questionnaire. First, the questionnaire results were tested by the use of a second sample of 17 eastern institutions, which provided us with information on key questions. The responses from this second sample were virtually the same as for the 41 institutions studied. (The responses from the 17 institutions in the second sample are, of course, not included or reflected in any way in this study.)

Second, the responses to the questionnaire in this follow-up study were those of top campus administrators, usually the president, chancellor, or members of his staff. They are not the views of disinterested observers, but they are nonetheless, we think, entitled to full credibility. These are the men and women who have told us when institutions

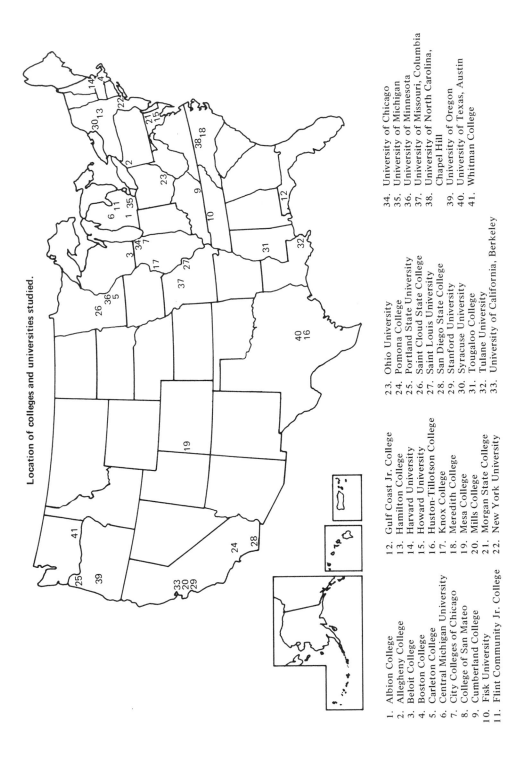

Location of colleges and universities studied.

1. Albion College
2. Allegheny College
3. Beloit College
4. Boston College
5. Carleton College
6. Central Michigan University
7. City Colleges of Chicago
8. College of San Mateo
9. Cumberland College
10. Fisk University
11. Flint Community Jr. College

12. Gulf Coast Jr. College
13. Hamilton College
14. Harvard University
15. Howard University
16. Huston-Tillotson College
17. Knox College
18. Meredith College
19. Mesa College
20. Mills College
21. Morgan State College
22. New York University

23. Ohio University
24. Pomona College
25. Portland State University
26. Saint Cloud State College
27. Saint Louis University
28. San Diego State College
29. Stanford University
30. Syracuse University
31. Tougaloo College
32. Tulane University
33. University of California, Berkeley

34. University of Chicago
35. University of Michigan
36. University of Minnesota
37. University of Missouri, Columbia
38. University of North Carolina, Chapel Hill
39. University of Oregon
40. University of Texas, Austin
41. Whitman College

falter and on whom the burden has been fixed. Now, when things seem just a bit better, they would be justified should they incline to give themselves a measure of credit.

BRIEF OVERVIEW A return check on the campuses whose financial conditions were reported in *The New Depression in Higher Education* reveals that, whatever the validity of the charge that neither exhortation, rebellion, or a new outside world can make colleges and universities change, it is now clear that a shortage of money can. The 41 schools in the study are changing. The changes are occurring in response to the pressures of difficult financial circumstances. For the most part, these changes cannot be identified with one or two especially significant decisions nor is there usually a moment in time when one can say they first began. They were probably already started in varying degrees in various institutions when the data for *New Depression* were gathered. More accurately, these changes are the results of a continuous process.

In some institutions that process is going on faster than in others, but in most of the 41 institutions the process has gone far enough in the last two years to permit us to identify its main elements that are significant for this study: Beginning with increased administrative and faculty awareness of the cost-income squeeze, there develop new managerial practices and organizational relationships. Their short-run consequence has been a sharp reduction in the rate of growth of the institution's expenditures. Although the need to cut expenditures motivated the development of these new managerial practices and organizational relationships, their influence extends well beyond questions of money. Questions of money eventually lead to questions of purpose, and these new managerial practices and organizational relationships form the evolving system by which the schools are making the transition from money questions to purpose questions. The additional consequence of these new practices and relationships, therefore, is the development of new administrative and faculty standards of judgment about educational quality and purpose.

In two years this process has moved fast enough so that what was then "unthinkable" (e.g., modifying the tenure system) is now becoming a credible experiment.

We shall consider the significance of these changes—in attitudes and awareness, in expenditures, in managerial practices and organizational relationships, and in standards of judgment—in subsequent chapters. For now, in describing the situations at our 41 institutions, it is clear that these changes have been effective in the short-run in slowing down and perhaps even halting eroding economic conditions. In almost all of the 41 institutions, the gap between expenditures and income is no longer widening: in most the gap in fact appears to be closing, and in some the gap has been eliminated. Although the institutions have been aided by some factors external to them, such as the reduced rate of inflation discussed in Chapter 4, the primary factors in this somewhat improved situation have been internal, the efforts of the campuses themselves.

As a consequence, there is among campus administrators more optimism about the financial future of their institutions than one could have predicted two years ago. It is a guarded optimism, and with good reason, for it is based on rather fragile conditions.

The most obvious finding from this look at the 41 institutions two years later is that most seem to have achieved a stabilized financial situation. It is fair to say that most (though not all) have gone from a financial condition of steady erosion to one of fragile stability.

It is important to emphasize how fragile the stability is, for, as we shall see, it is the produce of on-campus actions that cannot long continue to produce the same level of expenditure reductions as in the last two years; its future, therefore, depends increasingly on assumptions about events outside the campus and beyond its control. Many of these assumptions are themselves fragile. Hence, the guarded character of the administrators' new optimism. Moreover, not all institutions are enjoying this new stability. As we shall see, some continue to face deteriorating economic situations.

OUTWARD APPEARANCES OF STABILITY

Even before their financial status is known, the colleges and universities in this study, as elsewhere, present the outward appearance of stability. In the campus visits of May 1970, several institutions were operating while beset by student strikes and demonstrations. On two of the campuses, interviews about financial conditions were possible only after visiting interviewers were "cleared" by police. One interview was conducted in an administration building surrounded by chanting demonstrators. May 1970 was perhaps the peak period of campus protest about the Indochina war. This year, by contrast, the campuses do not face the problem of demonstrations and, as a result, administrators are able to give attention to their financial problems; indeed, many seem to be giving attention to little else. The campuses are quiet.

But, it is important to note, they are not *too* quiet. Each of the 41 institutions is still open and operating. From the perspective of two years ago, that is for some no trifling achievement. At the time of the interviews in 1970, administrators at several institutions talked confidentially about the possibility of being forced to close some operations, or an entire campus. For some, the lesser of these fears has come true, but all institutions are open and functioning. To the extent that survival is the test, all have made it.[2]

One method of dealing with adversity is merger. In the 1970 study, several interviewers were also told on a confidential basis (a promise not to identify the institution), that merger was being considered. In at least two cases, it was under very active discussion. But none has merged yet. Thus all 41 institutions still have the same names, with but two exceptions,[3] both unrelated to financial condition.

A further outward indication of the stable condition of the institutions is their enrollment, listed in the table on pages 12 and 13. Although nine institutions had smaller opening fall (headcount) enrollments in 1971 than in 1968, in only one instance was there clearly a substantial drop in full-time students. The overall enrollment picture is one of stability and modest growth.

Even the form of instability that is most visible—departure of the president or chancellor—does not suggest unusual instability among the 41 colleges and universities in our study. In the two years, turnover has been high but at approximately the level that is now normal for turnover of presidents.

Thirteen of the 41 institutions have a new president or chancellor since the original study in 1970. Listed alphabetically these institutions are:

> Albion College
> Carleton College
> College of San Mateo
> Flint Community Junior College
> Harvard University
> Morgan State College
> Saint Cloud State College

[2]William Jellema (1973, pp. 33-34) reports from his analysis of the Education Directory, 1971-1972, Higher Education, that "In 1970-1971, 40 private institutions either closed outright or merged with some other institution. Twenty-two of these were four-year institutions. Most, if not all, of these institutions appear to have ceased operating primarily for financial reasons."

A new study of the birth and death of colleges and universities sponsored by the American Council on Education (1972, p. 14) shows that although 133 colleges and universities founded since 1947 have closed, the number of new institutions being opened still exceeds the deaths.

[3]See notes on page 10.

San Diego State College
Stanford University
Syracuse University
University of California, Berkeley
University of Missouri, Columbia
University of Texas, Austin

From this list it is evident that the changes of president were made in each of the categories of institutions. New presidents preside at four national research universities, two regional research institutions, two each of the state and comprehensive colleges, the liberal arts colleges, and the two-year colleges. One of the five primarily black institutions has a new president.

Thirteen new presidents[4] means 32 percent of the total sample changed chief executives—a figure that suggests this group's experience is similar to recently published data on presidents of universities who are members of the Association of American Universities (AAU). AAU presidents currently have an average tenure of about six years.[5]

A more direct indication of stability is, of course, the assessment of those administrators responsible for the campus' financial and academic direction. When the administrators of the colleges and universities contrast the campus situation of 1972 with that of 1970, they report that progress has been made in dealing with their new financial circumstances.

ADMINISTRATORS' SUMMARIES OF THE CURRENT SITUATION

In the original study, the 41 institutions were divided into those we considered "not in trouble," "headed for trouble," and "in financial difficulty." The classification was a judgment based on the effects of financial condition on academic program and quality.

Following the campus visits in the original study, a synopsis of interviewers' notes was prepared for each institution, presenting a brief description of the financial situation and its operating effects; these were published in *New Depression*. In the present follow-up study, those brief published statements were submitted to administrators at each of

---

[4] A fourteenth presidential change is in process as this report is prepared for publication—that at the City Colleges of Chicago.

[5] In his article, "Presidential Discontent" (1970), Clark Kerr analyzes data on presidential tenure and summarizes as follows: "In 1899, the average years in office of this group of presidents (AAU institutions) was 10.9 years. By 1969, this had dropped to 5.9. The decline has taken place throughout the seventy years, but the big drops came in the 1930s, from 9.5 in 1929 to 7.7 in 1939; and in the 1960s, from 7.4 to 5.9. It appears that the average may still be going down. In 1969, 27.1 percent of the presidents had been in office less than one year, and 52.1 percent less than five years—in each case, the highest percentage in history. The comparable figures in 1964 were 2.4 percent [sic] and 38.1 percent and in 1899 they were 14.3 percent and 21.4 percent."

the institutions. Each was asked to prepare a current statement commenting on the earlier one and summarizing the current financial situation. These reveal something of the steps the campuses have taken in the last two years, as well as the consequences of those steps.

Designated "in financial difficulty" in 1971   Consider first the two sets of observations from those institutions that in 1971 were judged to be "in financial difficulty." An institution was judged to be "in financial difficulty" "if it had been moved by financial considerations to make cuts which, fairly judged, affect essential program *or* quality" (ibid., p. 91). Of the 41 institutions, 11 were judged to be in financial difficulty:

> Two-year Colleges:
> None
>
> Primarily Black Colleges
> Fisk University
> Huston-Tillotson College
> Tougaloo College
>
> Liberal Arts Colleges
> Beloit College
>
> State and Comprehensive Colleges
> Boston College
> San Diego State College (University)
>
> Leading Regional Research Universities
> New York University
> Saint Louis University
> Tulane University
>
> National Research Universities
> Stanford University
> University of California, Berkeley

Here is the synopsis of the interviewers' notes for each campus in 1970, followed by the administrators' current comments. It should be borne in mind that the current comments reproduced here comprise one answer to a questionnaire calling for 16 answers in all.

PRIMARILY BLACK COLLEGES

■ *Fisk University (original study)*   In 1970, Fisk carried a $1 million deficit. The endowment is being used up and will be gone in three to four years. This year the Afro-American Institute will be phased out. Several departments would have been eliminated were it not for deficit spending. Drastic across-the-board cuts have been made wherever possible. Construction has been cut back, and the number of faculty has been frozen at 90 for the last three years.

Fisk University (current situation) Fisk has eliminated the large operating deficit which it sustained in the latter 1960s, and its endowment is being replenished. The university was able to reverse its financial fortune through vigorous fund-raising, and with large grants from private foundations, the United Church of Christ, and several individuals. Strengthened management, with new personnel at the top and middle levels and with the introduction of modern management systems, has given the Fisk Board of Trustees new confidence in the future of the University. But the board and administration are concerned about long-term trends, for projections of Fisk's future financial posture are disturbing. The heart of the disturbance is the relentless character of cost rises in a small university which is proud of its fine heritage, good students, and excellent faculty, but which faces severe competition for students and faculty from the nation's wealthiest universities and most prestigious private colleges.

- *Huston-Tillotson College (original study)* Research has been cut back and the athletic program greatly reduced. Several faculty positions were eliminated. Further reductions have been made in intercollegiate athletic competition, music, and the number of course offerings. Insufficient income has necessitated cutting into the budget base. Despite cuts, the deficit of $55,000 for 1969-70 will grow to $95,000 in 1970-71. The number of course offerings has been reduced, and needed library expansion has been delayed. Efforts to pay competitive salaries have been stymied.

  Huston-Tillotson College (current situation) We did not incur a deficit for the 1971-1972 fiscal year. Church support has increased significantly. Enrollment has increased in each of the last two years. Although our budgetary situation is stable at the present time, long range commitments cannot be made unless the budget base is strengthened substantially.

- *Tougaloo College (original study)* The college, with an enrollment of about 700, is running a deficit between $300,000 and $400,000 with an endowment of only $500,000 and, at the time of the interview, was in arrears on current bills. Financial stringencies make it increasingly difficult to recruit qualified black faculty. Membership in various intercollegiate organizations has been eliminated.

  Tougaloo College (current situation) The college, with an enrollment of 750, is carrying a cumulative deficit of over $600,000 with an endowment of about $125,000. The deficit has been caused by the need to provide over $350,000 annually in unfunded student-aid (since the last report) to students from families whose income averages under $4,000.

If we can survive the next three years without lowering the quality of the institution, church funds, grant funds, improved foundation support, and improved management procedures will enable us to establish a sound financial future. We have proved to the society that we can produce graduates who can compete efficiently for new career opportunities recently opened to black-college graduates. We have sent an average of 40 percent of each graduating class to graduate and professional schools over the past three years (47 percent last year), including 30 medical students. This is a production record that funding sources cannot take lightly.

LIBERAL ARTS COLLEGES

- *Beloit College (original study)*   Administrators say that the college faculty is 12 positions below what it should be. The number of nonacademic employees has been reduced. For 1970-71, $100,000 has been cut from the total spent on student aid in 1969-70. The planned library budget allocation has been reduced. A planned American-studies program was postponed as well as an undergraduate tutorial program. Student research has been cut back. Performing arts programs and cultural affairs have been reduced.

  Beloit College (current situation)   An upturn in student enrollment and retention levels, plus increased current and capital gift income, and improved planning and cost control procedures have enabled the college to substantially improve its financial situation during the past two years and to protect it for the short-term future. Balanced budgets during the past two years have been accomplished without academic program cutbacks, and no further cuts in faculty or staff are anticipated. In fact, some programs previously threatened are being retained or expanded. New academic innovations are under way as part of a major refinement in the curricular program being inaugurated in the fall of 1972. The long-term financial stability and competitive position of the college will be dependent on (1) success of the current capital-fund campaign, (2) continued improvement in the current gift program, (3) continued attractiveness of the innovative Beloit program to students, and (4) a major public-policy shift in expanding educational opportunity by subsidizing the student so he can be free to choose his college on educational rather than financial grounds in place of operating government institutions at low tuition.

STATE AND COMPREHENSIVE COLLEGES

- *Boston College (original study)*   A badly needed library building has been postponed, and plans for dormitories have been cut back. Special admissions have been reduced. The percentage of graduate students has been frozen at the present level. Administrators are stopping the growth of faculty, despite the reservations of faculty and deans. The college carried a deficit in 1969-70 of $3.5 million and expects a deficit of $730,000 in 1970-71.

Boston College (current situation) The library building is still deferred, but a large dormitory project has been authorized and is being built and another one is planned. The sizes of the student body and of the faculty have been stabilized. The deficit for 1970-71 turned out to be $988,000. For 1971-72 a surplus of $10,000 is estimated in operating budget, but deficit spending continues in the capital budget.

■ *San Diego State College (original study)* Class size has risen. This year it was necessary to let 48 faculty positions go unfilled and to eliminate certain research positions. Sabbatical leaves have been cut in half. The equipment budget was cut by $20,000. According to school administrators, faculty and staff morale is low.

California State University, San Diego (current situation) Enrollments have continued to rise, with some increases in class size. There is a moderate improvement in the financial situation. Budgetary support has matched the increases in enrollment and cost-of-living, and recent salary increases have improved faculty and staff morale. Funding deficiencies continue in the areas of sabbatical leaves, equipment, and support staff.

LEADING REGIONAL RESEARCH UNIVERSITIES

■ *New York University (original study)* In 1970-71 the university will carry a deficit of over $5 million and will need to borrow to cover it. The university has partially offset its difficult financial situation by the sale of noneducational business assets. The number of faculty has been frozen and the number of teaching assistants reduced. Research has been cut back, and a moderate reduction has been made in the number of administrative posts. The student-faculty ratio will rise in 1970-71.

New York University (current situation) The estimated deficit for the academic year 1972-73 will exhaust the unrestricted endowment of the institution. The projected sale of the University Heights campus may replenish this. Proposed reduction of faculty and staff for the academic year 1973-74 and reduction in service costs will hopefully bring the budget into balance for the near term. Longer-term prospects, however, depend more on forces external to the university than on the efficiency of internal management.

■ *Saint Louis University (original study)* The School of Dentistry, the four engineering departments, and Parks College – a small affiliate specializing in aeronautical science—have been closed. Forty-five faculty positions were eliminated, and 40 permanent faculty members were consequently given two years' notice of severance from employment. The current allocation of the Medical School is one-third what it was three years ago. Library acquisitions and research programs were trimmed. Faculty salaries were raised only 3 percent—it is feared that some faculty may leave as a result. Many courses were postponed, and the student-faculty ratio has risen. The debate program has been eliminated for next year.

Saint Louis University (current situation) Substantial phaseout costs associated with the closing of the Schools of Dentistry and Engineering are behind us. In recent years operating deficits have been reduced, and a balanced budget for 1972-73 has been adopted. Cost-reduction programs are continuing—salaries have been frozen across the board for the coming year; all academic programs are being scrutinized and evaluated, including analysis of the income and expenses for each program; and needed building repairs have been posponed (although we know that the repairs will have to be made eventually and will probably cost more). We recognize that some of these programs are short-term, stopgap measures to buy the time needed for development of acceptable long-range solutions. If enrollment does not decline, we believe that with proper planning, the use of modern management techniques and a reallocation of our resources, we can achieve a turn-around in our financial condition, although it will be an uphill battle.

■ *Tulane University (original study)* The number of faculty has been frozen. This and increased enrollment have resulted in a higher student-faculty ratio. Cutbacks have been made in teaching assistants and research activities. Ph.D. programs were eliminated in the fields of classics, Italian, geology, music, theater, and social work. Maintenance has been deferred for many years, and the library budget starved. A cut of $100,000 was made from the speech and theater budgets. The laundry and printing press were eliminated.

Tulane University (current situation) This institution has been engaged for the past several years in a careful analysis, study, and review of all factors impacting its financial condition. It has chosen to decentralize the budgeting process, making each major division of the institution responsible to some extent for its own financial solvency and has disseminated financial information about the university as widely as possible. It has reduced faculty slightly, while at the same time increasing enrollment slightly, which has resulted in an increase in productivity. More significantly, perhaps, it has embarked on a program which, if successful, will place the School of Medicine on a self-sufficient basis, which in turn should make it possible for the entire university to operate on a balanced budget. The situation at this institution is still critical, but there is far more reason to be optimistic than was the case in 1970. Another plus factor has been the decrease in the campus unrest which characterized the situation in 1968-70. This has led to some direct improvements in terms of costs of insurance, etc., as well as indirect improvements in private philanthropy.

NATIONAL RESEARCH UNIVERSITIES

■ *Stanford University (original study)*   The university has cut $1 million from its original budget for 1970-71 but will still have a deficit of $1,427,000. Its budget planning requires that $2.5 million be eliminated in the next four years. Deficits are being financed from reserves. All unfilled faculty posts are frozen. A total of 21 faculty positions have been eliminated, although no tenured faculty members have been severed. Library acquisition growth has been cut. General funds have been withdrawn from the Hoover Institution and the Medical School. New programs in urban and environment studies are not being funded for the time being. Plans for library and law school building are on the shelf awaiting funding. The drama program was drastically reduced.

Stanford University (current situation)   The university has launched a $300 million five-year, fund-raising campaign, has begun several interdisciplinary teaching and research programs, and has increased its attention to and capacity in more effective management. Annual budget deficits have been reduced from $1,427,000 in 1970-71 to $600,000 in 1972-73, as part of a five-year plan to bring income and expense into balance by 1974-75. Budget reductions and income adjustments totalling $4.5 million have been made to date, $1.5 million more are contemplated. Specific faculty (39) and nonfaculty (48) positions have been eliminated, though others have been added, keeping the size of the faculty and staff approximately constant.

■ *University of California, Berkeley (original study)*   The student-faculty ratio is rising. One research institute in the social sciences has been eliminated. Seven other research units (including earthquake engineering and urban social problems) are forced to operate without a regular support budget. Others, such as an institute on race and community relations, are only partially funded. Administrators report that an "indeterminate number" of proposed new courses have been postponed, as have plans for development of a medical school. Some courses, such as freshman seminars, have been cut. The summer quarter was eliminated to save expenses; as a result, the state withdrew funding for 208 new faculty positions, most of them unfilled, that would have been required for year-round campus operation. Summer instruction will now have to be on a self-supporting basis. The number of graduate students and teaching assistants is being reduced. There are no capital funds. Plans for administrative growth were shelved and the number of administrative posts was reduced. Cuts have been made in community-service and various research programs. Administrators believe that the fact that faculty received no salary increase in 1970-71 has had an adverse effect.

University of California, Berkeley (current situation) The student-faculty ratio is now 17.0 (compared with 15.0 in the late 1960s). This is among the highest in the nation for a major public research university with doctoral responsibilities. The student-TA ratio has worsened similarly. Graduate enrollments have been reduced 15 percent. Two high-cost specialist departments and one research institute have been terminated. Two major computers have been taken out of service. Library service has been reduced. Student services and administrative services have been trimmed and rationalized. An appreciable number of low-enrollment courses have been eliminated or are scheduled less frequently. The size of sections in required freshman courses has been raised by an average of 5 percent, and evening laboratory schedules have been initiated. New programs and program changes are authorized only when long-run financing is assured by eliminating or reducing some other activity. Experimental programs are controlled rather strictly on this basis. The administration has been radically reorganized and stream-lined. Limits have been set on community-service and research programs. Financial aid programs have leveled-off.

On the other hand, the freeze on faculty salary increases has been lifted (with 9 percent approved for 1972-73). The institution has also made some radical interprogram shifts of support that have served to sustain its principal programs. Resources are now reasonably well adjusted to revised program objectives and priorities. Operations have been adapted to available resources without serious loss of quality, and the impetus to seek new initiatives has been sustained. If the present fragile resource base is not further eroded (by inflation, or by transfer of resources to finance expansions on other UC campuses), the evidence indicates that the institution can maintain the standard of its programs, and meet needed new responsibilities, even with its present reduced standard of living.

These responses remind us that although the 11 institutions had a common designation in the 1970 study, they have important differences in their problems and in their approaches to solutions, as well as in their size, character, and academic mission. Yet along with these differences the responses of these institutions reveal important similarities. They all cite some relative improvement, at least about some aspects of their financial situation. Although it is due to a number of factors, that improvement is mostly a function of the institution's own efforts. The problem and possibilities for each are becoming clearly identified and defined. They are optimistic, partly due to success in efforts to deal with their problems, and partly, it seems, due to their awareness itself and to the fact that they are taking action. Each is concerned about the longer-run trends. As we shall see later in this report, they have good reason to be concerned about the longer run.

Designated "headed for financial trouble" in 1971 Let us examine next the responses from the 18 institutions which, at the time of the original study were judged to be "headed for financial trouble." At the time of the campus visits, we concluded that "these 18 colleges and universities were able to meet their current, self-defined responsibilities without reducing quality." All had made cuts, but these were judged not to affect quality or essential activities. The basis for categorizing these schools as "headed for trouble" was the judgment that they "cannot expect to continue to meet current standards and maintain program or they cannot ensure support for existing planned program growth. Their income and expenditure prospects are such that they can now confidently predict a time in the near future when they will have to increase income substantially or cut expenditures so much that program or quality will be revised downward."

The 18 institutions are:

Two-year Colleges
   City Colleges of Chicago
   Mesa College
Primarily Black Colleges
   None
Liberal Arts Colleges
   Albion College
   Allegheny College
   Carleton College
   Cumberland College
   Knox College
   Pomona College
State and Comprehensive Colleges
   Central Michigan University
   Portland State University
Leading Regional Research Universities
   Ohio University
   Syracuse University
   University of Missouri
   University of Oregon

National Research Universities
Harvard University
University of Chicago
University of Michigan
University of Minnesota

Here are the administrators' current comments, bringing up to date the original study's summary of their schools' condition. Again, it should be remembered that these comments comprise only one of a number of responses to the follow-up questionnaire.

TWO-YEAR COLLEGES

■ *City Colleges of Chicago (original study)* Administrators believe that the colleges will not be voted additional tax-levy authority. Most administrators are certain that they could not win a referendum. At present, Chicago has a very small rate of increase in assessed valuation. The colleges have taken on a number of partially funded, low-priority programs. There have been some campus disturbances, and security costs have risen (from $100,000 to $250,000 in one year). Some legislators don't like the name "Malcolm X College" given to one of its units. Inflation, and the great pressure for new programs, particularly in community service and black studies, have pushed costs up sharply. Some new administrators were inexperienced. The faculty union has become militant in resisting administrative efforts to cut costs by reducing the number of faculty members (not by firing, but rather by not filling as many vacancies).

City Colleges of Chicago (current situation) Available financial resources are short by 10 percent to meet the fiscal needs of the normal operating expenditures, which forced us to reduce a number of nonteaching positions as well as nonteaching expenses. The rate of decrease in available revenue per FTE student has been accelerated.

■ *Mesa College (original study)* Income is becoming fixed as costs continue to rise. Administrators see no chance of an increase in the mill-levy authority or in the state formula for allocating faculty salary support. Any further raises in fees would place Mesa in a noncompetitive position, and it would have to borrow heavily because of lack of reserves. The only chance for flexibility is to increase enrollment, a difficult task given the fact that Colorado has opened seven new junior colleges in the last three years. Minor campus disturbances have had some effect on private gifts. The number of bids for insurance dropped from 15 to 2 in one year. The computer has become a large financial factor which may grow. The need for salary increases is a major cause of the seriousness of the situation. Federal student aid funds have been cut. A $100,000 federal reimbursement for vocational programs was allocated by the state to the *state* system. The federal work-study program has been cut.

Mesa College (current situation) The full impact of the financial squeeze is now being felt at Mesa College. Despite sizable reductions in certain areas of expenditures and continued deferral of needed capital improvements, this institution is forced to planned deficit spending for 1972-73. The revenue base is relatively fixed, with great resistance from property owners for any increase in the mill-levy. Tuition rates are competitive with other Colorado community colleges and the prospect of an increase in the state funding rates is poor. With a decline in the total number of high school graduates coupled with the opening of several new Colorado community junior colleges in recent years, Mesa College may experience a decrease in enrollment for 1972-73. However, with the addition of baccalaureate degree services in the fall of 1974 and prospects for general population increases in the area, we anticipate a growing demand for our educational services. With more imaginative use of the many educational influences that exist in society outside the formal school and college programs, we should be able to cope successfully with the cost problems.

LIBERAL ARTS COLLEGES

■ *Albion College (original study)* Ford program funds ran out in 1970, and by 1971 college reserves will be gone. Student aid costs are massive (the college is currently spending $900,000 annually). Enrollment may not hold. Inflation is affecting gift receipts. College officials are unsure that people are going to continue to be willing to pay for private higher education. Other important cost factors are: rising costs and inflation, a higher level of expectation on the part of the faculty, and decreasing respect of students for property (resulting in higher maintenance costs). Officials are worried about the unknown cost consequences of the knowledge explosion.

Albion College (current situation) Careful examination produced an optimum enrollment of 1,550 full-time-equivalent full-fee-paying students. The college believes this enrollment can be achieved continuously with high caliber entering freshmen. A new professional management program, individualized curriculum; higher levels of assistance from alumni; reduction in administration, faculty, and staff size, seem to augur well for the future. All future buildings will be constructed only after funds are available to endow the cost thereof. Attention is being given to large, peripheral expenditures: computer, food service, utilities, etc. Cost reductions can be made without seriously truncating services.

The corner to good fiscal health seems to have been turned.

Careful management can save private higher education. Wasteful practices must be abandoned. Curriculas will have to be streamlined and be more responsive to career objectives, without becoming narrowly vocational. Student-faculty ratios must increase as innovations in teaching and learning become practical. Cost control must be central to planning and operation, not in a repressive sense, but in a discriminating value-judgment sense. If inflation can be kept below 5 percent per year, and college income can increase 5 percent per year, sound programs and fiscal operations are within reach.

- *Allegheny College (original study)* Campus unrest has caused a great deal of antagonism in the locality. The climate for higher tuition and larger giving has deteriorated. The endowment is growing at a slower rate. Administrators believe that continued tuition increases will result in changing the composition of the student body. Pressures to enroll more disadvantaged and foreign students are rising and increasing commitments to minority students are very costly. The Pennsylvania Scholarship Fund is in difficulty. Security and insurance costs will rise substantially. Because of a strong possibility of collective bargaining, costs might become even more fixed. There are no funds for an urgently needed library building. The college is in a bad financial squeeze. It had to put all available funds into an arts and music building, a project too far advanced to stop, despite fund shortages.

Allegheny College (current situation) The college appears in a sound position with an underlying uneasiness. A balanced budget both this year and next appears assured. There is no floating debt and the cash position is satisfactory. Alumni giving rose sharply in 1971-72 and constituency attitudes toward the college have improved. External sources of student aid funds are slightly less uncertain. However, three consecutive declines in the number of admissions applications gives us genuine concern. The program for the disadvantaged is proving very costly and will not plateau until 1973-74. Finally, a recent study shows there is negligible "fat" in our budget, now leaving us with few alternatives in the event of financial stringency.

- *Carleton College (original study)* Expenses are rising more rapidly than income. Foundation grants are running out. Student aid is in serious trouble because costs for financial aid and student services are increasing so rapidly. Federal aid is falling off. Gifts are not increasing as fast as expected, partly due to the decline in the stock market. Although there have been few campus disturbances, they may have affected giving.

Carleton College (current situation) Operating budgets are in balance. We have a long-term program for strengthening financial condition by increasing enrollment while maintaining faculty and staff constant and by initiating a major capital-fund drive. A deficit in the student-aid budget continues to grow, but federal and state programs, if fully funded, should help offset this trend.

■ *Cumberland College (original study)* The only realistic possibility of increasing income is to increase fees. To do this, the college would have to recruit heavily from outside the area, because Appalachian families would no longer be able to afford the costs. Therefore, the purpose for which the school was intended would not be served. Already, the financial-aid budget is inadequate. During the recent period of federal aid to higher education, the Kentucky Baptists did not allow Cumberland to obtain federal building money. Enrollment may decline because of out-migration from mountain counties and the proximity of two public junior colleges. Tightness in federal student aid funds is beginning to hurt. College officials want to expand in the area of community service, but foundations are not favoring this type of institution.

Cumberland College (current situation) The balancing of the operating budget of the college is going to be a continuing problem, but the trustees and college administration do not believe this is insurmountable. Operating income can in some measure be increased by advancing the charge to the student, keeping this annual advance comparable to the percentage rise in costs generally caused by inflation. The combined charge for room, board, tuition, and fees has been and is extremely low. It is competitive with the similar charge at tax-supported colleges and universities.

Gift support, other than that provided by the constant amount supplied annually by the Kentucky Baptist Convention, has increased gradually over the past five years. Up to the present, none of this last-mentioned annual income has been used for current operations. Since a moderate percentage of this income is unrestricted, this amount can be used for operations, if necessary. While following this practice might slow down the rate of construction of physical facilities, this, in itself, would not be extremely harmful to the institution and its program.

The only debts the college has now are carried on recently constructed buildings and the total of these debts is from 1/6 to 1/7 of the worth of the college. Included here is the unpaid part of the cost of a building erected since the [original] Carnegie survey. By following the present schedule, one of the debts will be cleared in three years and each of the others in five to six years. This schedule can be followed even if part of the annual gift income is used for operations.

In summary, while the balancing of the operating budget will continue to be a problem in the foreseeable future, the trustees and administration of the College do not believe this is a problem which will bring about the demise of the institution, nor do they believe that to solve the problem the original purpose of the institution must be abandoned. Funds are being procured for additional buildings.

Since Cumberland College serves so many students of limited means and since a large number of these must have total aid, if the recent bill passed by the Congress of the United States is funded within the next year, it may not be necessary for the College to use any of the annual gift income for operations other than that supplied by the Kentucky Baptist Convention.

■ *Knox College (original study)*   Reserves are down from $1,200,000 to $250,000. The growing quality of the University of Illinois is being felt. College officials believe that, even though there have been no major disturbances on campus, Knox has nevertheless been hurt in the eyes of private donors. They fear that the parents of this generation may become still more unwilling to underwrite an expensive education. Insurance and security costs have increased, but the most important additional cost is the staff time and energy spent attending to or anticipating campus disturbance problems. The knowledge explosion has created problems in financing computers and the library. Since the rate of inflation exceeded predictions, Knox is spending more on student aid than it had expected.

Knox College (current situation)   The college has cut costs and its financial situation is pretty much under control. Reserves have been depleted; cost cutting has been severe. Costs are under control.

■ *Pomona College (original study)*   Rising costs are the primary concern. Administrators report increased expenditures now and in the future for student-aid and minority programs, computer and library resources. Last year reserves were used for student aid. Next year they will have to start using general college funds. Student aid and counseling funds are not adequate to allow Pomona to admit significantly more minority students, although there is pressure to do so. Pomona has a substantial deficit. Until recently the college has been able to afford relaxed management. Administrators do not agree on whether, if the situation worsens, the president has the power to move the students-to-faculty ratio significantly upward.

Pomona College (current situation)   Pomona College was listed as an institution headed for financial trouble in *The New Depression in Higher Education*, although it was admitted then that the college probably could also be placed in a healthier category. The primary concern in 1970 was the increasing cost of minority education and rising demands for student aid. With the full operation of the minority programs, the college seems now to have achieved a degree of stability within manageable limits. Because of the fortunate growth in funds for student aid, the college still has not exhausted its reserves and has still not had to use general college funds for student aid purposes. This is a tribute not so much to skillful management as to the generous provisions for financial aid by supporters of the college.

Nevertheless, constant reliance on increasing tuition income has come to be questioned, because it is not at all certain that market resistance to high-tuition private institutions can be avoided. There has been a reduction in the applicant pool although the college is still able to be highly selective in its admissions policies.

The rate of growth of costs suggests the need for a major capital-funds campaign to increase the endowment of the college in the middle '70s, and plans are under way to develop such a campaign. The college has been successful in increasing unrestricted giving over the last several years.

There are no plans at present for major changes in the educational program of the college, particularly in respect of the present student-faculty ratio which has been allowed to change upward only slightly in the last two years; it has not been significantly altered since 1970.

In short, Pomona College has good prospects unless there is a significant change in public attitudes toward private higher education in the United States.

STATE AND COMPREHENSIVE COLLEGES

■ *Central Michigan University (original study)* Administrators are concerned whether the university is well regarded in the public mind. Legislative budget cuts reflect a growing hostility to higher education. Past surpluses are used up. The tax base is inadequate. The only flexibility possible is that which would come from enrollment growth. The decline in the auto industry at the time of the interviews was having an important effect on state schools. Campus disturbances have affected the conditions for raising income and probably were a significant factor in this year's budget cuts. Rising increased-cost factors include police (up 100 percent in two years); a sharp increase in the number of separate departments caused by the knowledge explosion; student pressure to diversify faculty and courses; and reduction of federal spending for student aid.

Central Michigan University (current situation) Our administrators are somewhat more optimistic than they were two years ago—largely because of relatively more favorable treatment from the legislature. The fundamental problems remain, however: The tax base of this state is still inadequate, the automobile industry rests on a fickle base, and welfare costs are spiralling at the expense of allotments for higher education. One aspect of the total problem has actually deteriorated—the student enrollment pressure has lessened, depriving the university of the money that would normally be produced by an expanding student population. Many unpopular decisions will have to be made within the next two to three years.

- *Portland State University (original study)* The present political climate in Oregon reflects substantial resistance to additional taxes and changes in the tax structure. Administrators believe student unrest is the most significant depressant factor in Oregon. The university is seriously understaffed and lagging behind in library books and equipment. The administration has been starved for support. Inflation-impact problems are serious with respect to equipment, books, supplies, utilities, maintenance, computers, and salaries. Student-aid costs and tutoring costs have increased. Generally, programs expanded at a great rate, but support, including salaries, was neglected.

  Portland State University (current situation) Compared to two years ago, the current financial situation is significantly worse. Prospects are that the financial condition will become tighter. Portland State University's situation is spare, but not sick—after a year of financial exigency.

  LEADING REGIONAL RESEARCH UNIVERSITIES

- *Ohio University (original study)* The climate for obtaining additional funds is very poor in Ohio. Administrators report that the legislature disapproves of campus protest activities and appears to have lost confidence in education as the solution for society's problems. Rapid growth in the 1960s was not accompanied by adequate planning: The library has been seriously undersupported; insurance rates have increased greatly; the university has a heavy load of deferred maintenance. The nonacademic employees' union is pressing hard for wage increases. Federal support has fallen off. Fees are as high as they can go. Enrollment cannot be raised. Campus disturbances will have a strong legislative impact that has not yet been felt because, at the time of the interview, the university was in the two-year budget.

  Ohio University (current situation) The climate for obtaining additional funds continues to be very poor in Ohio, even though a state income tax that was voted in last year boosted funding for higher education. The ex-Chancellor of the Board of Regents disclosed on June 26, 1972, a plan for refinancing higher education that recommended a drastic shift in funding from the state to the student, with relatively low fees at two-year institutions and extremely high fees at four-year institutions. The General Assembly increasingly regards higher education as an endless drain on state resources and apparently is seeking every avenue to minimize direct subsidy to the campuses. Insurance rates have increased greatly, the university has a heavy load of deferred maintenance, educational quality has eroded, and the dormitory system is in trouble financially because of overbuilding and changed student lifestyles. The state has acknowledged pressure from nonacademic employees by putting through a series of increases in civil-service wages, only part of which have been funded by separate appropriation. Federal support continues to fall off. Fees have been raised each year and the state system as a whole maintains one of the highest fee structures of any in the nation. Enrollment is close to the statutory ceiling, but there are indications that the number of freshmen may decrease and produce a drop in income. The financial picture for the university is thus deteriorating on all counts.

■ *Syracuse University (original study)*   The university has been deferring maintenance, but it is no longer able to do so. It is rapidly approaching an upper limit on tuition. Improvements are needed in library, computer, and research facilities. The university has suffered from cutbacks in foundation and federal support, and administrators fear cutbacks in state support as well. Endowment, which is small, is being used to meet deficits. Changes in tax regulations, the stock market decline, and campus disturbances have had significant effects on private giving. Campus budget reallocations will become more necessary as "catch up" expenditures are made for items that were deferred in the past.

Syracuse University (current situation)   The university still has an uneasy financial position, aggravated by reduction in reserves because of recent deficits and by borrowing to meet capital needs. However, the outlook is more favorable than it was two years ago.

The university has achieved a balanced operating budget through an increase in enrollment and in tuition as well as through cost reductions. Once-feared reductions in foundation, federal government, and state government support did not materialize to a significant degree. The university now has a new library and improved computer facilities. Capital funds are urgently needed to repay debt incurred to pay for unfunded portions of new buildings and for maintenance deferred in the past. Such funds are also needed to improve research facilities and to refurbish the space released by the academic units that move to new buildings.

■ *University of Missouri (original study)*   Because the public voted down an income tax increase and the governor and the legislature are stalemated, the school will receive the same amount from the state in

1970-71 as it did in 1969-70 (with a student enrollment increase of 1,700). Recent necessary fee increases have made fees higher than average. The legislature appropriated no university construction funds in 1969 or 1970 (except for an urgently needed power plant addition). Already there is a serious space shortage. In addition, the university has been required to build and operate a medical school in Kansas City. The outlook for legislative support is bleak at least until 1973-74. This economic deterioration is attributed to inflation, decline in the national economy, federal budget cutbacks, taxpayer backlash, and the general loss of confidence in higher education. There have been some student disturbances, and the university has been affected by a public mood of retaliation against students and universities. According to administrators, Missouri is forty-third among the states in per-capita taxes paid to the state government. Missouri higher education finds itself in growing competition with other public service needs (public schools, conservation, mental health), and the university is experiencing growing competition from state colleges. The effects of federal cutbacks in research, construction, and student aid funds are beginning to be felt. Enrollment pressure continues. In the years ahead, the university will be very hard pressed in plant maintenance and improvement. There is virtually no chance of raising the needed money to meet increased minimum needs resulting from projected increases in enrollment. Salaries need to be improved (but this could only be done this year by raising tuition). There are also many unmet library needs that must compete with very high computer and data-processing costs.

University of Missouri (current situation) Since the data were gathered for the original study two years ago, state appropriations have fallen considerably short of university requests and needs. Although the national weighted-average percentage gain in appropriations of state tax funds for operating expenses of higher education in the 50 states, between 1969-70 and 1971-72, was 24.25 percent, the comparable figure in Missouri was 17 percent. Among the states, Missouri ranked in the relatively low position of 35-36, tied with Vermont.

Austere budgets of 1970-71, 1971-72, and 1972-73 have developed an extreme attitude of frugality and concentrated efforts toward program review and cost reduction. Through rigorous review of the budget base and existing programs; careful scrutiny of personnel positions and freezing many of those that became open; increasing workloads; and sharply reducing expenditures for library materials, physical plant maintenance, and equipment acquisition and replacement, the trimming has reached the bone. This process has gone considerably beyond healthy dieting. The need to accrue a significant additional amount of forced savings has begun to show cumulative and pernicious effects. The situation has been compounded by the lack of state funds for new building purposes. At the same time, the purchasing power of the dollar continues to erode, program quality deteriorates, faculty and staff salaries lag, workloads increase, classes become larger with classrooms more crowded, and the university faces stiffer and stiffer competition in pleading its case for additional financial resources. It was in the face of these mounting problems that the university, with great reluctance, was required to raise student fees for the academic year 1972-73.

■ *University of Oregon (original study)* The university is facing cuts, recommended by a consulting firm, which the firm assumes can be easily made by trimming off "fat" and improving efficiency. Administrators anticipate a decline in federal research funding. The 1960s expansion was not accompanied by sufficient growth in support, especially for library and administration. The state has not changed its tax base significantly. Administrators report that campus disturbances have been damaging to the university's ability to obtain budgetary and other significant support. The legislature may be favorably impressed with California's recent denial of requested faculty salary increases. Administrators believe that the current nationwide economic situation has caused Oregon to suffer a somewhat steeper drop than the economy as a whole, particularly because of the decline in residential building, which adversely affects Oregon's large lumber industry.

University of Oregon (current situation) This year marks the definite end of a growth period and the beginning of a serious downturn in growth and, with it, an accentuation of problems. Federally funded programs are being curtailed or abolished at the same time that state support is diminishing. Increasing reliance is being made on higher tuition payments and recruitment of students.

NATIONAL RESEARCH UNIVERSITIES

■ *Harvard University (original study)* Costs are increasingly relentless. During the 1960s, operating costs rose at the average of $12 million a year, due much to inflation. Federal support is declining. Arts and Sciences is operating at a deficit. Cutbacks have severely weakened the School of Education, School of Design, and the Divinity School. Other parts of the university–Public Health, the Medical School, the Division of Engineering and Applied Physics, and several other departments–are being threatened. Federal fellowship and traineeship cutbacks are serious. Much more student aid will be needed. Computer and library costs are rising rapidly. Student and faculty aspirations are increasing, and unless the funding situation changes, they cannot be met.

Harvard University (current situation) Although feeling many of the fiscal pressures common to major private research universities, most notably those of inflation, Harvard is in a sound financial position. Its $1.35 billion endowment and reserves remain intact. The Faculty of Arts & Sciences, which is in the process of absorbing additional costs associated with the Radcliffe semi-merger and student body expansion as well as with the reduction of outside support for graduate students, is operating at a deficit projected to turn around without invasion of capital in a three-year period. Tuitions are still rising and will be financed in part by increasing student loans at each of the highly decentralized schools within the university. Library costs are going up faster than income, but other cost-income relationships are stabilizing. Some new programs are going forward on a restricted priority basis, but in a context of caution with respect to the uncertainty of external support, both federal and private, and to the still-changing environment in the economic-support and manpower-demand levels in various areas of graduate and professional education.

■ *University of Chicago (original study)* The budget has been balanced recently only by using the Ford Challenge grant, which will probably be used up this year. Government funds have leveled off. Because of a heavy shift toward reliance on federal money in the 1960s, the university is extremely sensitive to changes in federal spending. It is heavily committed to graduate instruction and, therefore, prospects for cutting costs are dim. A large deficit is expected again in 1970-71 that will this time necessitate using endowment principal. At that point the school would have reached what its administrators describe as "a critical financial situation." Student fees are nearing the ceiling. One prospect administrators see for meeting increased costs is substantially increased private giving—and this has been affected by inflation and campus disturbances. The university is under great pressure to finance day-care centers. It has recently moved heavily and expensively into community service. Campus concern with pollution resulted in conversion from coal to gas at a cost of $2 million per year. The cost of security is significant and has doubled over the past two years. The student-aid budget will probably decrease. Computer costs have risen rapidly. The new library will be extremely expensive to operate.

University of Chicago (current situation) In addition to the several actions that have been taken by the university to enhance the flow of income, there have been serious attempts over the 1969-72 budget period to bring expenditures within the academic budget under better control and to reduce their rate of growth. The policy on holding faculty size constant has been successful. The attempt to relate restricted expenditures (which have been to a large extent under the control of the academic units) to unrestricted funds in such a way as to enhance the use of the latter has been effective. Reviews of academic activities that might be eliminated or reduced without harm to the quality of the university have had modest success. Similarly, there has been some success as a result of the steps taken in various academic areas to stimulate student recruitment and to rejuvenate the Summer Quarter. December 15 and March 15 reviews of faculty reappointments have sharpened as budgets have tightened and recommended new appointments have undergone more critical scrutiny with reference to both need and quality. Auxiliary enterprise budgets have been brought into better balance, especially those relating to undergraduate housing, and expense and equipment budgets have been reduced. The latter, along with budgets in support of library services, may have reached a level that threatens serious academic deficit. In the largest and most complicated area of the university—the Biological Sciences Division and the Pritzker School of Medicine, along with the several hospitals and clinics—expenditures have been brought under essentially "line item" control, with centralized "oversight" to an extent that goes well beyond the traditional practices of the university and which, under normal circumstances, might be seriously questioned as the best way to "administer" this university.

While much of the above might be viewed as having the characteristics of a "plan," we have not, as has been the case in some other universities, thought of it or announced it as a plan to reach some pre-set goal with reference to the size of the academic budget by a given point in time. We have tried, rather, to look at the primary dimensions of the academic budget and to make decisions in concert with the deans in such a way as to introduce as few and as gentle perturbations into the university as possible, and yet meet the fiscal reality of the period. We have had in mind as the primary goal the conservation of the University of Chicago as a unique institution of higher learning.

- *University of Michigan (original study)*   Inflation and a poor outlook in the auto industry will be reflected in state support of the university. Administrators say the outlook is dismal. Next year, it will no longer be possible to keep budgetary savings. The university is suffering from a critical lack of capital funds and, simultaneously, is subject to new demands in areas such as ecology. The problem of how to support students from low-income families is becoming acute, both because of increased commitment and because charging higher fees is the only major possibility of increasing income. Federal support for hard sciences has dropped. Administrators foresee federal cuts in research, fellowships, and student aid. Although at the time of the interview campus disturbances had not yet had direct effects on appropriations, administrators believed there would be an effect.

University of Michigan (current situation)   The financial situation has stabilized somewhat from two years ago, although there has been no increase in real dollars for university operations since that time. Inflation is still a problem and a serious shortage of funds for student aid exists. University reserves in the educational budgets have been used up and these budgets must now be in balance within resources available.

More capital funds are available today as state support for capital projects has improved considerably. A shortage still exists in funds for equipment replacements, laboratory renovations, and library books.

The drop in federal support for graduate students is serious, and strenuous efforts are needed to restore these funds by the Federal Government or replace them by gifts from foundations, individuals, and other sources.

A significant effort is under way to obtain participation by faculty and student groups in the use of funds, in the evaluation of programs, and in planning long-range strategies for growth and development.

■ *University of Minnesota (original study)*   Federal cutbacks have begun to affect the university severely in several areas, and because of the decline in the economy, administrators see little chance of improving gifts and endowments. Accelerated development of other types of educational institutions has increased competition for state monies (junior colleges, in particular, are growing in favor). Withdrawal of federal funds for local projects aggravates the local need for state tax resources. Federal traineeships have been reduced. The Medical School, underfunded by the state, has become overly dependent on federal funds. Costly efforts have been undertaken to reduce environmental pollution. Computer costs have skyrocketed. Student-aid funds are inadequate to meet the growing need caused by a greater university commitment to the disadvantaged. Campus disturbances thus far have had no apparent effect on appropriations, but backlash in the state is real and may be felt in the next legislative session. The public is losing confidence in higher education. Reapportionment may hurt the university, since it has traditionally counted on support by the rural legislators, whereas punitive bills have come from the urban legislators.

University of Minnesota (current situation)   Federal cutbacks continue to affect the university, especially in the area of the health sciences where the Medical School continues to be underfunded by the state. Efforts to correct the situation are slow and painful—resources from other parts of the university gained from retrenchment have been reallocated to the health sciences. Economies in industry have had an adverse effect on fund-raising efforts. The proportion of gifts from industry has been decreasing the past several years. People in Minnesota, as in other states, are witnessing a taxpayers' revolt. The Governor and the Commissioner of Administration are advocating no new taxes for 1973-75, which means a status-quo budget. It appears that few new program requests will be funded, and salary increases and other formula increases will be held to a minimum.

Student-aid funds are still in short supply, especially freshman scholarship funds. Campus maintenance and building maintenance are being reduced and deferred and campus-wide awareness campaigns are being waged to conserve utilities. The university lost some favor with the last legislature over such items as airplanes, faculty salary levels, expense accounts, investments, retirement plans, etc. There are some indications that the issues are not dead and again will be used as a reason for not appropriating funds to the university, although improved information and work with the legislature may well avoid many of the problems seen in recent years.

These responses from administrators on the "headed for trouble" campuses reveal a combination of work and hope. All show the effects of the financial problems, and all have made adjustments. None is fully confident about future financial status, because of their necessary dependence on conditions over which they have no control. It is obvious that their stability is fragile. Not surprisingly, the responses to the financial situation of institutions in this category seem less drastic than those at the schools in the preceding category, and, again not surprisingly, there seems to be a relatively clearly identifiable split here between institutions whose condition continues to deteriorate and those whose condition seems to be improving.

Designated "not in financial trouble" The uncertainty about the future, evident enough in the responses from the 18 institutions just considered, is even more evident when one looks, two years later, at the 12 institutions found in *New Depression* to be "not in financial trouble." These institutions were judged "not in trouble" because the original study found they were able to meet their current self-determined quality and program standards and could, with some assurance, plan new program growth. At the time of that study, these schools had not made program cuts nor abandoned existing plans for future programs because of financial difficulty. It was noted then that, although these institutions were not immune from the cost-income problem facing the other institutions, they were in a better position than the others and could be more confident about the future. Twelve colleges and universities were judged "not in financial trouble." These were:

Two-year Colleges
    College of San Mateo
    Flint Community Junior College (Genessee)
    Gulf Coast Community College

Primarily Black Institutions
Howard University
Morgan State College

Liberal Arts Colleges
Hamilton College
Meredith College
Mills College
Whitman College

State and Comprehensive Colleges
Saint Cloud State College

Leading Regional Research Universities
University of North Carolina, Chapel Hill

National Research Universities
University of Texas, Austin

In the original *New Depression* study no individual statement was published concerning these institutions. In the follow-up study, their questionnaire included the following:

After our visit to your campus in 1970, we concluded that as of that time your institution was "not in financial trouble." This judgment was based on the observation that your institution was able to meet its current program standards, and could with assurance plan program growth. We would very much appreciate your assessment of the current validity of this conclusion.

Reproduced below are the administrators' responses to this request (which was one of the 16 questions asked):

TWO-YEAR COLLEGES

■ *College of San Mateo (current situation)* Our financial condition is reasonably secure based on current factors of inflation and assessed valuations for the rest of the decade.

■ *Flint Community Junior College (Genessee) (current situation)* We do not characterize our financial condition as "in trouble." We do have sufficient funds to meet the costs of present programs. Where our money is in short supply is in the area of educational support; that is, we would do a good deal more by way of tutorial programs and special helps for the disadvantaged student if additional funds were available.

■ *Gulf Coast Community College (current situation)* Again—no problems.

PRIMARILY BLACK INSTITUTIONS

■ *Howard University (current situation)* Howard University has financial problems as indicated in reply to previous questions [showing a deficit for current operations and need for more plant and equipment]. However, these problems do not imply a "crisis situation" with impending serious consequences. Our current programs are progressing but the improvements sought for are impatiently awaited. The planned program growth for the future is going forward with assurance that financial support will be forthcoming. The planning is encouraged by the cooperative review and support given to the proposals of Howard University.

- *Morgan State College (current situation)* When we compare Morgan with other institutions, especially those that are privately funded, we are "not in financial trouble." In other words, we do not face the financial crisis or depression that has gripped other institutions. We still have needs that are unmet: student aid, capital development, and special funds for compensatory education.

LIBERAL ARTS COLLEGES

- *Hamilton College (current situation)* Our institution is still not in financial trouble. We probably will not be in the near future if our coordinate institution, Kirkland College, becomes financially independent. Although Hamilton created Kirkland College, it is independently chartered and has its own board of trustees and administration. It graduated its first class in 1972. It has leaned heavily on Hamilton for financial aid in its first four years of operation. We are expecting it to become financially independent within the next two years. If our expectations are realized, Hamilton should not be in financial trouble. If Kirkland College does not achieve financial independence, Hamilton might well find itself in financial trouble.

- *Meredith College (current situation)* The financial stability of the college can be maintained if enrollment continues at optimum and gift income is maintained. The significant and continuing denominational support has been a major factor in the financing of this institution, and the institution has been greatly benefited by unprecedented voluntary support in recent years as a result of an aggressive fund-raising program. Significant increases in student charges and carefully planned increases in enrollment have produced revenues necessary to meet the college's planned program of improved benefits and support of the academic program. Finally, sound business practices and techniques have created financial stability and an atmosphere of cautious optimism.

We are fully cognizant that our current posture could drastically change if any of these basic conditions should not continue: (1) Optimum enrollment of 1,200 full-time students. (2) Voluntary support of approximately $750,000 annually, including $260,000 from the denomination. (3) Utilization of sound business practices including cost analyses procedures.

- *Mills College (current situation)* There is never enough money. An economist can quickly prove financial doom. On the other hand, financial difficulty has been a way of life for the past 100 years, and this will undoubtedly continue to be a way of life for a small, private, liberal arts college. Mills College is in financial difficulty primarily because enrollment increases have not materialized. We are still anticipating that fall 1973 enrollment projections will materialize.

- *Whitman College (current situation)* We have, since 1970, introduced new academic majors, increased salaries, and increased student financial aid. No programs have been eliminated. We have the normal concerns. Like everyone else we are on a treadmill of rising costs, fear of increasing tuitions, fear of competition from tax-supported institutions, and knowledge of the increasing gap between tuition and costs. We are in the midst of a (so far) successful campaign to increase endowment but we have also been obliged to increase tuition annually at a rate roughly equal to inflation.

STATE AND COMPREHENSIVE COLLEGES

- *Saint Cloud State College (current situation)* There has been no appreciable change, with the possible exception of faculty salaries. In fact, several programs (faculty-improvement grants and faculty research) have been improved.

LEADING REGIONAL RESEARCH UNIVERSITIES

- *University of North Carolina, Chapel Hill (current situation)* State funds should be sufficient to meet our short-range objectives. Future is uncertain due to reorganization of higher education in the State of North Carolina.

NATIONAL RESEARCH UNIVERSITIES

- *University of Texas, Austin (current situation)* This institution can operate for one or two more years with essentially level funding without significantly decreasing service and without an adverse effect on the quality of the academic programs. Beyond two years, however, we see very serious problems if state and federal support do not overcome the erosion of inflation and permit the university to maintain its commitment to excellence in programs and services.

Although most of the institutions retain their financial stability, during the last two years several show evidence (and others the fear) of a weakened financial condition. If the same standards of judgment were used today as were used in *New Depression*, some of these schools might be considered "headed for trouble" and others would be close to that category. The majority of the 12 institutions in the "not in trouble" category are still not in trouble, however.

In addition to asking the administrators for descriptive summaries of their current financial condition, the follow-up questionnaire asked them to indicate how the current financial condition of their institution compared with that of two years earlier—the time of the original study. Each responded. The summary below records the results, but it is not precisely a summary of the responses. The categories below are based on our judgment, which in most, but not all, cases corresponds with the responses. Our judgment is based on the entire questionnaire (especially Questions 1, 3, 9, 13, 15, and the administrators' summaries), and its comparison with the results two years earlier.

TABLE 2   Current financial condition compared with that of two years ago

Not as good	*About the same*	*Better*
City Colleges of Chicago	Boston College	Albion College
Hamilton College	Flint Community Junior	Allegheny College
Howard University	College	Beloit College
Mesa College	Gulf Coast Community	Carleton College
Mills College	College	Central Michigan
New York University	Knox College	University
Ohio University	Meredith College	College of San Mateo
Portland State University	Morgan State College	Cumberland College
Saint Cloud State College	University of North	Fisk University
University of California,	Carolina, Chapel Hill	Harvard University
Berkeley	Saint Louis University	Huston-Tillotson College
University of Chicago	Tougaloo College	Pomona College
University of Minnesota,	University of Michigan	San Diego State College
Minneapolis	Whitman College	Stanford University
University of Missouri,		Syracuse University
Columbia		Tulane University
University of Oregon		
University of Texas, Austin		

Believers in an ordered world will find little comfort in the above summary. Some institutions of each type endured a relative decline in their financial situation, and at least one of each type enjoyed improvement. In all, 15 are not in as good financial condition as they were two years ago. Fifteen seem to have improved their financial condition. Eleven are judged to have held their own. Of course, these categories are crude; within each of these categories is a variety of experience, and some institutions within the "not as good" and "better" groups have experienced considerably more change than others in the group.

When we look at this grouping by the categories of financial difficulty used in the original study, we find the following. Of the 12 judged "not in financial trouble" in the original study, five have slipped, six are in about the same condition, and one is in an improved situation. Among the 18 found "headed for trouble," eight improved and eight slipped. Only two remained the same. Of the 11 considered "in financial difficulty," six are better off, three are the same, and two are in a somewhat poorer position. These listings are summarized in Table 2 below.

Most of the reasons for the foregoing judgments appear in the excerpts from the individual institutions given above. Almost all are based on the effect of expenditure reduction, further efforts at cost reduction, enrollment estimates, expectations about salaries, hopes about the consumer-price index, possible state action (more than federal), and private giving.

EDICTED TRENDS
1972-1975

Administrators at each institution were asked to assume that the trends now under way in the cost and income variables at their schools would continue. What, each was asked, would be the effect on your institution in three years?

This attempt at a three-year forward look is summarized in Table 3 below. Administrators at all 41 institutions responded, and their responses are grouped into two categories—those for whom the situation would presumably continue to deteriorate, and those for whom the situation would remain relatively stable. Two schools indicated that the situation might improve slightly, but since none saw a substantial improvement in prospect, a category for improvement is not needed and these two schools are listed as "about the same." Thus, of the 41 institutions, 23 indicate that their situation would be "about the same" if present trends continue, and 18 believe it would be "not as good."

When one compares the individual institutions' estimates of their future condition (assuming present trends) with their estimate of their change in condition over the past two years, one finds the following. Of the 15 institutions whose current condition is "not as good" as it was two years ago, 12 believe that their condition would be still worse in three years. Of the 11 whose current condition is "about the same" as two years ago, four believe their condition would be "not as good" three years from now if the situation continues unchanged. Of the 15 whose condition is "better" than it was two years ago, only two believe it will be "not as good" if present trends continue.

INTERPRETATION
OF THE ABOVE
VIEWS

Any interpretive judgments made from the above data describing the new depression two years later are subject to considerable qualification. The number of institutions is relatively small and, as is noted fully in the original study, they were chosen as illustrative of types of institutions, not as a representative sample of all institutions. Moreover, the

TABLE 3   Current financial condition compared to that two years ago, by categories in original study

			Category in original study		
Not in trouble			*Headed for trouble*		
Current situation			Current situation		
Not as good	*Same*	*Better*	*Not as good*	*Same*	*Better*
Mills College	Morgan State	College of San Mateo	Mesa College	U. Michigan	Cumberland College
Howard Univ.	Whitman Coll.		U. of Missouri	Knox College	Cen. Mich. Univ.
Hamilton Coll.	U. of North Carolina		U. of Chicago		Carleton Coll.
U. of Texas	Gulf Coast Jr. Coll.		U. of Oregon		Albion Coll.
St. Cloud State Coll.	Meredith Coll.		U. of Minn.		Pomona Coll.
	Flint Comm. Jr. Coll.		Ohio Univ.		Syracuse Univ.
			City Colls.-Chicago		Allegheny Coll.
			Portland St. Univ.		Harvard Univ.

TABLE 4   Predicted financial condition three years from now (if present trends continue)

Not as good	*About the same*
Two-year colleges	
City Colleges of Chicago	College of San Mateo
Flint Community Junior College	Gulf Coast Junior College
Mesa College	
Primarily black colleges	
Howard University	Fisk University
Huston-Tillotson College	Morgan State College
Tougaloo College	
State and comprehensive colleges	
Portland State University	Boston College
	Central Michigan University
	Saint Cloud State College
	San Diego State College

In financial difficulty		
Current situation		
Not as good	*Same*	*Better*
U. of Calif.	Tougaloo College	Sanford Univ.
New York U.	Boston Coll.	Beloit Coll.
	Saint Louis Univ.	Tulane Univ.
		San Diego State Coll.
		Fisk Univ.
		Huston-Tillotson Coll.

Not as good	*About the same*
Liberal arts colleges	
Carleton College	Albion College
Knox College	Allegheny College
Mills College	Beloit College
	Cumberland College
	Hamilton College
	Meredith College
	Pomona College
	Whitman College
Leading regional research universities	
New York University	Saint Louis University
Ohio University	Syracuse University
University of Missouri, Columbia	Tulane University
University of Oregon	University of North Carolina, Chapel Hill
National research universities	
University of California, Berkeley	Harvard University
University of Michigan	Stanford University
University of Minnesota, Minneapolis	University of Chicago
University of Texas, Austin	

two-year time period is a short one for generalization. There are other limitations. The financial problems, as we noted in the original study, are varied. They vary by types of institution and by situation and therefore are not easily aggregated. In short, there are several types of financial problems, not just one. Moreover, any judgment of financial conditions rests on assumptions about the future. In a situation where the facts are changing, and where the standards of judgment are also changing, predicting tends to be hazardous.

Since a major study will soon be under way by the National Commission on the Financing of Postsecondary Education, our judgments may be offered safe in the knowledge that they will be put to national test in about one year. No one should be misled for long.

Given the limitations, what generalizations seem warranted from the above data?

1   The basis for rejoicing over the more stabilized current situation is quite limited. It is, for some institutions, a situation of genuine stability, but there is also continued downward movement for an equal number, and in some cases, there is serious financial trouble ahead. Although no institution predicted outright bankruptcy in the next three years, three, and possibly a fourth, could be in grave circumstances if present trends do continue. Moreover, there are no policies external to the campuses that have dramatically helped improve the situation and that can be relied upon.

2   The above responses and the individual institutions' record of expenditures suggest that, on the whole, private institutions are in somewhat better control of their situations than the public institutions. Certainly their administrators tend to be more optimistic. Partly this is due to the fact that the rapid growth in the public educational sector has ended. For some public institutions, support formulas are beginning to work in reverse. In several parts of the country, states are revising their policies of low public tuition. An end to aggressive growth of public institutions and the beginning of higher tuition ease the competitive problems, at least in prospect.

The evidence is slender, but it suggests that private institutions may be doing more about both expenditure and income problems than are public institutions. This could be attributed in part to greater motivation of institutions faced with less stable income sources, but in greater part it may well reflect their greater freedom of action. One encounters repeated complaints from public institutions about the constraints on their uses of funds.

One by-product of easing the competition over enrollment and price between public and private institutions is a change in the argument as to why public policy should be concerned for private institutions.

Whereas the argument was once heavily based on the need for diversity in educational experience, it seems now to be increasingly based on the idea that it is cheaper to extend capacity through the underutilized private sector.

3 Although the private institutions are as a group more optimistic, there are greater extremes of financial condition in the private sector than in the public. The private sector includes institutions that seem the most secure and the most vulnerable. There are secure institutions among all types, but the type that seems in the relatively best position is what is often called the "highly selective" liberal arts college. Not all of them are secure, but as a group, they have been able to gain better control of their position than the others.

Among the private four-year institutions that do not fit into that "highly selective" liberal arts category, there is a wide variety of experience. Some are in fairly strong financial position, others are quite marginal. Almost all private institutions carry a high student-aid burden, and those typically carrying the highest burden, the institutions in cities, are subject to other high urban costs as well. There is no clear pattern for the primarily black colleges. They reflect the above forces and therefore the category includes some institutions that are relatively secure and some that are quite vulnerable.

4 Within the public sector, the two-year colleges are often thought to be a relatively favored type of institution. The responses from the follow-up study do not tend to support that view.[6] The inference they most easily permit is that the state colleges feel most secure. The research universities see themselves as the most threatened of the public institutions.

5 As a group, the research universities seem to be in the greatest state of concern about their future. The public institutions are somewhat demoralized about the qualitative leveling to which they fear they will be subject. The private universities, even those financially secure, have doubts about their future as research institutions. This is a fear borne of restrictive federal policies toward funding graduate education and toward science, especially basic research. The federal budget proposed for fiscal 1974 phases out hospital construction grants, regional medical and community mental health center programs, training grants of the National Institutes of Health and National Institutes of Mental Health, social work training programs, capitation grants to schools for veterinarians, optometrists, and pharmacists, and institutional support for

---

[6] The original study "idicate [d] that, in recent years, the . . . public two-year colleges ha[ve] had the greatest protection against the cost-income squeeze. . . ." (1971, p. 47), n. 3). The public research universities were in disfavor there, too.

schools of public health and allied health fields. Elimination of these programs presents serious new financial setbacks for most large universities. The University of California system, for example, estimates that over a three-year period it faces the loss of $80 million as a result of these program cuts. New York University, already under great pressure to bring its books into balance, suddenly faces an additional deficit of several million dollars in its medical facilities due to these proposed changes. These are not special examples. All research universities with major medical facilities are facing similar problems.

6   Administrators at institutions of all types endorse expanded student-aid programs and believe their institutions would benefit from them; but, relatively few believe that expanding student aid alone will solve their institution's financial problems. Research, service, plant, and other institutional needs, especially in the more complex institutions where tuition is a smaller percentage of income, are not met by student aid and related cost-of-education grants.

7   Finally, it is difficult to interpret the financial conditions of colleges and universities, even with the help of their detailed assessments, for a fundamental reason: The present condition of stability is very fragile. Let us look at the quality of the current stability in more detail.

4. Fragile Character of the Current Stability

In the view of college and university administrations, worry about the future tends to overshadow their sense of relief that some stability has been won. Given the recent past, university administrators would be cautious in any event. No doubt that explains in part their anxiety about the future. But there are reasons more important than prudence. Thus, in answer to the question in the follow-up study, "Have you found that modern management techniques for planning and decision making are helpful in solving your cost-income problems?", administrators at most institutions gave cautious responses. The administrators indicated that, while such methods, along with more traditional good management practices, can produce savings, they alone will not solve the problem.

The most important reasons for the cautious outlook are first, that the current stability has been achieved largely through extraordinary cuts in expenditures that clearly cannot go on indefinitely; and second, because the current stability is dependent upon assumptions about the external situation that are uncertain and beyond the schools' control. Let us examine each of these in turn.

SEVERITY OF EXPENDITURE CUTS As we found in *New Depression*, the earliest response to the cost-income squeeze included efforts to control costs. At the time of the original study, these were in a tentative, marginal, or beginning stage — ranging from belt-tightening to worrying. What this follow-up study shows is that cost control has escalated to an extraordinary degree.

A considerable part of the reduction in expenditure growth has been achieved by holding down the increase in faculty salaries[1] and by deferring maintenance. These methods of economizing set in motion con-

[1] In its Report on the Economic Status of the Profession, 1971-1972, the American Association of University Professors states: ". . . the shrinkage in funds devoted to faculty salary increases has been greater than the retardation of price increases, and we are forced, *for the fourth year in a row*, to report that the change in the economic status of the profession is worse than it was a year ago" (*AAUP Bulletin* 1972, p. 178).

ditions that in time tend to increase costs. Not surprisingly, most administrators mention that they need more funds for salaries and for building maintenance. Since these are costs that cannot be deferred indefinitely, administrators clearly have a sense that they are living on borrowed time.

The fact that the current limitation on expenditure growth cannot go on indefinitely seems confirmed if we look at higher education costs over a much longer term than our two-year period.

As a result of the great advertising campaigns of savings banks, devoted straphangers in public transportation and TV watchers know that, thanks to the wonders of compound interest, money invested at 6 percent doubles in just 12 years. This fact has not escaped opera-goers, whose $5.50 seats have risen to $11.00. Least of all has it escaped the notice of academic administrators, whose costs have more than kept pace with the opera, and for much the same reasons. A labor-intensive activity that has no demonstrable productivity gains to offset rising costs makes an increasing claim on resources. Total current fund expenditures for higher education represented 1.1 percent of the gross national product in 1959-60; by 1971 it was 2.5 percent, and at the rate of increase for the 1960s, would reach 3.6 percent by 1981.

In the spring of 1967, then Provost William Bowen of Princeton found that the expenditures of Princeton, Vanderbilt, and the University of Chicago revealed an interesting pattern. He found that for several decades expenditures for instruction and departmental research rose at the remarkably constant (compound) annual rate of 7.5 percent per student.

That 7.5 percent figure is often called "Bowen's Law," honoring not only its discoverer, but also the fact that it seems so fully applicable to the recent experience of higher education. In the original *New Depression* study, expenditures for instruction and departmental research per student rose in the decade of the 1960s at the average of 7.3 percent per student per year for schools "not in trouble," 7.7 percent for those "headed for trouble," and 8.0 percent for those "in financial difficulty." Although this group of institutions was not "representative" of the nation as a whole, it is remarkable how closely the experience of our institutions approximates that predicted by Bowen's Law.

In a study for the Carnegie Commission, June O'Neill showed the extent to which educational costs rise more rapidly than increases in the consumer price index. Her data show[2] that for the period 1929-30 to 1959-60, costs (per credit hour) rose 2.5 percent faster than the

---

[2]O'Neill (1971, pp. 61, 62, 68). See also Carnegie Commission (1972, p. 35, Table 5). Cost data used include public service, libraries, student services, administration, etc., as well as instruction and departmental research.

average increase in the consumer price index. In another study, the Carnegie Commission staff estimates that during the 1960s educational costs per FTE student in higher education as a whole rose at an annual average rate that was 3.4 (or depending on the precise period and the method used, 3.3) percent higher than the rate of increase in the consumer price index.[3]

Alarmed by the implications of that rate of expenditure growth, the Commission recommended that institutions cut back to the "historic" rate of 2.5 percentage points above the rate of inflation. In its report *The More Effective Use of Resources*, the Commission asserts "The central thrust of this report is that the total institutional expenditures of higher education must be, should be, and can be reduced. . . ."

This follow-up study shows that these institutional expenditures *are* being reduced. Expenditure growth for these 41 institutions has been sharply cut. Here are the figures: Expenditures per student for the institutions rose during the period 1966-67–1969-70 at the average annual rate of 8.1 percent.[4] This period included the last of the "Golden Years" and the beginning of the downturn, thus the average rate of expenditure growth exceeded what might be called "O'Neill's Law"– expenditures rise 2.5 percentage points per year faster than the consumer-price index. The average increase in the consumer price index for the period 1966-67–1969-70 was 4.2 percent. Thus expenditures per student rose at the average of 3.9 percentage points above the consumer price index.

In the period since the first study, colleges and universities have achieved a marked reduction in this rate of expenditure growth. For the period 1969-70–1972-73, the institutions report an average expenditure growth of only 5 percent per student per year. During that same period, the average annual increase in the consumer price index was 4.5. Thus the difference was a remarkably small 0.5, or one-half of one percentage point above the increase in the consumer price index.

Three of the institutions actually had a negative rate-of-expenditure growth for the period. Their total dollar expenditures per student declined. In 17 of the schools, expenditure growth was less than the increase in the consumer price index. Their real dollar expenditures per student declined.

---

[3] See Carnegie Commission (1972, p. 36). The cost data used include public service, libraries, student services, administration, etc., as well as instruction and departmental research.

[4] Expenditures here and in the follow-up study questionnaire are defined as "current operating expenses (*excluding* sponsored research, student aid, and auxiliary enterprises)." These categories of expenditure in the follow-up study are thus roughly equivalent to those of the O'Neill and Carnegie Commission studies. See notes 1 and 2, this chapter.

How bleak this level of expenditure is becomes apparent when we compare it to expenditure rates described in three previous Carnegie Commission reports dealing with expenditures. The comparisons are summarized in Table 4 below.

Have Bowen's Law and O'Neill's Law been repealed during the last few years? It seems unlikely, but for the moment, on many campuses their writ is not running.

One of the questions in this restudy asked academic administrators to assess the validity of the Carnegie Commission's recommended economies, which the Commission proposed in order to achieve the 2.5 growth rate over the rate of inflation. The responses tend to support the Commission's view that this limited level of expenditure growth is possible and could be lived with. But it appears from the expenditure data that at least for the short run that recommendation has been overtaken by events. The institutions are in fact living with expenditure growth rates that are well below the Commission's recommended restrained growth level.

TABLE 5   Follow-up study expenditure rates compared with earlier studies

	Rise in average annual education expenditure over average annual percent general inflation
Average expenditure growth rate per student, 1966-67–1969-70, institutions in *New Depression in Higher Education*	3.9
Average expenditure growth rate per student, 1959-60–1970-71, *The More Effective Use of Resources**	3.4
O'Neill finding on expenditure growth rate per credit hour 1929-31–1959-60† and Carnegie Commission recommended expenditure growth rate per student‡	2.5
"Rock bottom" growth rate policy described in *New Depression in Higher Education* §	1.0
Actual expenditures 1969-70–1972-73 per student, restudy of institutions in *New Depression in Higher Education*	.5

SOURCES: **The More Effective Use of Resources*, p. 36.
†*Resource Use in Higher Education*, pp. 61, 62, 68.
‡*The More Effective Use of Resources*, p. 4.
§ *New Depression in Higher Education*, p. 112 (based on total current fund expenditures including student aid).

It is important to understand the limitations of these new findings about expenditures. They are based on data from 41 institutions, with complete data for the full period from 36. They reflect changes for a short period. They are compared in the preceding discussion with data measuring slightly different categories of expenditure. Like the current severe fluctuations in the birthrate, these follow-up data must be interpreted with caution. Short-term expenditure-per-student figures are influenced by changes in enrollment, and it is not easy to isolate the precise extent to which they are due to policy. Thus, although the largest reductions in growth rate occur in the public institutions and in the institutions judged "not in trouble" in the original study, without further corroboration the data do not warrant interpretive judgments about these two groups of institutions.

The data do, however, justify two observations: First, it is clear that for this period at least, the schools are operating at sharply reduced rates of expenditure growth. Second, given the findings of previous studies, this level of operation cannot continue for a very long period without serious adverse consequences to some of the institutions. The Carnegie Commission's proposed rate-of-expenditure growth can perhaps be lived with, but the current severe level of cutting—which, as we indicate above, defers faculty salary increases and maintenance costs, among other things—cannot.

ASSUMPTIONS ABOUT THE EXTERNAL SITUATION

Inflation   The second reason administrators believe that the essential character of the stability is fragile is that its future depends in good part on assumptions about external forces over which the campus has little or no control. The most obvious of these is price stability. The decline from an average annual price increase of almost 6 percent in 1970, to one of under 3.5 percent in 1972 was an important factor in helping the colleges and universities recover some stability in their financial situation.[5] There is no price index for educational institutions, but it is known that their costs rise faster than the consumer price index. The prices of inputs of colleges and universities—books, laboratory materials, supplies, and equipment—all rise faster than the weighted average of prices of the items in the consumer market basket, most of which the college also buys. Estimates of the size of this difference vary. Administrators report from informal campus studies that they believe that their costs rise up to one and one-half times the consumer price index. Thus the drop in prices in 1971 and 1972 may have had a different effect on academic institutions than could be predicted from

[5]The calendar year percentage increases in the consumer price index for the period used in this study are: 1966=2.9; 1967=2.9; 1968=4.2; 1969=5.4; 1970=5.9; 1971=4.3; 1972=3.4.

the consumer price index alone. But as the economy enters Phase III, there is general concern that a sharp increase in prices, especially in the face of lagging salaries, would be predictably very serious. In fact, in February 1973, the first month of Phase III, consumer prices rose 0.8 percent—a seasonally adjusted annual rate of 9.6 percent—the largest price jump in 22 years.

Trends in voluntary support The recent stability is also based in part (as the earlier excerpts from the schools' responses indicated) on a recent upturn in private contributions to colleges and universities. Given the fact that in previous years private contributions suddenly dropped, there is reason to be worried that such a situation might occur again.

According to estimates prepared by the Council for Financial Aid to Education, the dollar amount of voluntary support of colleges and universities rose each year in the 1960s until 1969-70, when it dropped by an estimated $40 million. Much of this drop was due to the sharp decline in corporate support of higher education—from a high of $375 million in 1969 to an estimated $340 million in 1970. This drop is ascribed to the drop in corporate earnings reported in that year, which no doubt also influenced personal giving.

In addition, deferred giving (life income trusts, annuities, etc.), which began to decline in 1967-1968, continued to decline through 1970-1971, no doubt because the Tax Reform Act created uncertainties about the tax consequences of these transactions.

The overall upward trend in voluntary support was reestablished in 1970-1971. The statements from some of our 41 institutions reflect this upward trend. Although it was important in specific instances, the upturn in giving amounts to a relatively small increase in overall income for the 41 schools. The Council for Financial Aid to Education estimates that total voluntary support has risen to the new high of $1.860 billion, an increase of 4.5 percent over the previous year's figure, and some $60 million above the previous 1968-1969 high. Corporate giving rose to $356 million, an increase of 1.5 percent over 1970. According to Curtiss E. Frank, President of the Council, as of mid-1972 "there are indications that aid to education by business is once again expanding, but much needs to be done to make up for lost ground." (Council for Financial Aid to Education, 1972, p. 5)

Enrollments Still another reason that the current stability is fragile is, as the administrators' assessment noted in the preceding chapter indicate, its dependence on stable or slightly increasing enrollments. Given the sudden leveling in enrollment nationally, these aspirations will be difficult for some institutions to achieve. For the private institutions, enrollment is coming increasingly to depend on public policy—another element in the uncertain situation. In the study, administrators were asked to assess the likely future impact of the Higher Education Amendments of 1972 on their situation. Very few expect it to be of much help in the near future, although many believe it could be helpful if it were fully funded.

State aid   Since there is little expectation that much federal money will be appropriated and spent, state policy actions seem to have more bearing on the stability of the institutions for the short term (*Trends in State* . . ., 1973). Such state aid could take the form of increased assistance to students as well as to institutions. In the last two years, more than one-third of the states have instituted or expanded direct or indirect aid to private institutions. But, it is also now reported that the proportion of state budgets going to higher education has stopped growing; and that in two-thirds of the states, the proportion of the budget going to higher education is actually declining (*Chronicle* . . ., 1972, pp. 1, 2). Thus the prospects of a dramatic change in state support seem unlikely, both to public and private institutions.

5. Bases for the Current Stability: Institutional Change

Although the new financial stability is admittedly fragile and may prove to be short-run, it is nonetheless an important achievement. Seen from the campus perspective of two years ago, even this possible short-term stability seems remarkable. How did it come about? To some extent, as we have just seen, it was helped by off-campus factors. Yet the expenditure figures make clear this stability is primarily the result of internal efforts. And indeed, that is what administrators say. The follow-up questionnaire asked: "To what extent and in what ways is the difference between your present situation and that of June 1970 due to external differences? Internal differences?" The great majority indicate that improvement was due to internal factors.

It is also evident that the sharp expenditure reductions cannot be isolated from other changes. What the entire questionnaire reveals is that institutional changes are occurring that make possible the kind of expenditure reductions that produced the stability. As we noted at the outset, there is under way a process of change, and it is the main agent of the new stability.

CHANGE IN HIGHER EDUCATION? Given the prevailing views about the lack of change in higher education, it seems almost a bit audacious to suggest that there are changes occurring that could have important consequences. The matter may be clarified somewhat if we acknowledge at the outset that when we observe the details of what is happening on campus we see little drama and little action responsive to the "change" literature of recent years. What is happening on campus is not inspired by the visions of change educational reformers talk about. No grand academic design is being followed. No commanding pedagogical ideal informs the main actions being taken. Rather, what we see under way is the painful but undramatic process of adjusting operations and aspirations to relatively poorer financial circumstances. For most institutions, poor financial circumstances still mean a reduced rate of income growth inadequate to match steady or growing rates of cost increases. But for some, it means no income growth in the face of rising costs.

Some changes in program or staff made in response to pressing financial circumstances have been the object of publicity. Thus, the sale of New York University's Height's campus, or the notice of layoff of faculty members, as is now underway in the state college system in Minnesota, are the subject of public notice and discussion. Their effects are real and their impact on the individuals involved, painful. There is ample reason to believe that despite the apparent stability, and in some ways because of it, more of these painful adjustments will occur. Ironically, however, as they become a more common occurrence, their visibility will diminish.

A few of the constructive ideas and programs produced by this adjustment process have commanded some public interest. Among these ideas and programs are the deferred tuition plans at Yale University and Duke University, the Beloit College income-related tuition plan, and the Common Fund for educational endowments. But most of the work of adjusting academic institutions to more stringent circumstances involves devices unlikely ever to capture the popular imagination—budgetary control programs, management information systems, retrenchment and reallocation devices, priority and planning committees. More often than not they tend to be regarded primarily as technical matters, not unimportant to be sure, but generally not primarily related to the basic missions of education. They are likely to be regarded as changes that facilitate the educational process, and not matters that are likely to define or seriously influence it. These changes, made in response to financial stress, are poor nominees for historification.

At the outset we noted that these changes are more accurately seen as part of a continuing process—a process with two main elements: First, a change in attitudes that grows from an increased awareness by staff and faculty of the cost-income squeeze; and second, the development of new managerial practices and new organizational relationships. Let us look briefly at each of the particular elements in the process.

ATTITUDES One troublesome finding reported in the original *New Depression* study was that "most colleges and university officials believe that their view of the financial troubles is generally not shared by others off campus or on" (1971, p. 14). In only about one-half of the 41 colleges and universities did top administrators believe that "the faculty has a good understanding of its financial problems." Somewhat fewer (about 40 percent) reported that "students have some awareness of the school's financial situation."

It is not a wish for ideal "communication" that makes this situation troublesome. A lack of shared perception is a problem because of the very nature of academic institutions. Colleges and universities are complex organizations of professionals. Peer judgment is an essential ingredient for their most important decisions. Student judgment is becoming an increasingly important part of decision-making procedures. In these circumstances, it is difficult, if not impossible, to make hard planning and operating decisions in response to financial problems when conditions are generally not perceived as serious. Since most academic planning is done several years in advance, this situation can be especially troublesome. Plans continue and obligated funds are spent; planned buildings are built, even though there is no budget for their operation once completed. As of 1970, this was the case on several campuses in the study.

The lack of a shared sense of economic stress was observed in a 1937 study conducted by the AAUP. That study found that institutions of higher education carried on for about two years without making expenditure adjustments, which in retrospect, it appears they could and should have made. After the crash in 1929, there was little evidence of awareness and response by 1931-32. The authors wondered, why did that two-year lag have to occur? (See American Association of University Professors, 1937.)

Our data are insufficient to become the basis for a lag theory, but they are clearly adequate to warrant the conclusion that for the institutions in this study, the awareness gap found in 1970 is closing. The responses from our 41 institutions indicate that in the intervening two years financial stress and the decisions it has made necessary have produced on campus an awareness of rising costs and their implications. In response to the question "In what ways has the financial stringency had beneficial impacts on your institution?", all but five of the institutions reported that in various forms it had increased understanding and awareness of costs; that it had a profound impact on attitudes. Every institution but one reported that financial stringency affected attitudes. All but five reported that, in some way, stringency had also affected them favorably. The most frequently mentioned effect of the financial stresses on campus was that of making faculty, students, and staff members more aware of costs. It seems ironic, but increasingly true, that the consciousness enveloping campuses these days, is cost-consciousness. It may not qualify for "Consciousness IV," but it is the state of mind that is succeeding "Consciousness III."

When the statements on changes in campus attitudes from this return study are analyzed, four main points emerge.

Awareness The first and most obvious element of the new attitude is, as already noted, the awareness it has produced. Beloit College responded: "We know more about every dollar we spend than we ever did in the past. The faculty and staff are more alert to the realities of the cash flow within the organizations." That view, if not always so concisely put, is expressed by most of the institutions. There can be little doubt that people on the campus are becoming accustomed to taking cost problems into account. Students know about financial problems through higher tuition bills, larger classes, and shorter library hours. Budget problems are now a frequent front page story in student newspapers. The Chairman of the American Council on Education noted in her opening address to the 1972 council meeting that these days academics are heard from primarily on matters of money. What they lack in money, they now have in awareness.

Expectations The second aspect of changed attitudes is their apparent effect on expectations. They are down. The questionnaires report that the awareness of financial problems had had an effect on attitudes about building. "It has made us less building happy" is one report. Other typical responses: "It has eliminated the development of esoteric programs"; "We adopt no new programs, unless they are cost-beneficial." What these and similar comments reveal is that the rising expectations common to a boom period on campuses have come down with the new financial realities. "We have been forced," reports Portland State University, "to face financial realities."

A concern that this process of reduced expectations may have future adverse consequences is expressed in the response from Harvard University, which notes that financial stringency has the effect of sacrificing innovation and imagination. It "sacrifices the future for the present. Future constituencies are unrepresented." A similar concern was expressed by the response from the University of Chicago: "masochism is not a good philosophical framework for a scholarly institution." Thus, although there are mixed concerns about its future impact, no one debates the fact that expectations have changed.

Climate conducive to change The campus responses reveal a third aspect to these attitude changes—they create a climate conducive to change. It may be, as just noted, that the reduced expectations tend to short-change future generations, but at the same time, there is developing a willingness to change. This view is well expressed in a faculty speech to the academic senate, sent us by one of the institutions in the study.

... we [faculty] are responsible, by Regental delegation of authority, for educational policy, while the administration is responsible for resource allocation.

When times were easier and money was more readily available, we each could proceed with our delegated responsibilities relatively independently of the other, although Budget Committees routinely complained that they weren't consulted about budgets and administrators routinely complained that they weren't consulted about courses and curricula. Times no longer are easy and money no longer is readily available, and our two functions no longer are independent or even very separable. Every decision about resource allocation today directly and immediately affects, and in some cases determines, short and long term educational policy, and every decision about educational policy has implications for present and future resource allocation.

It is certain that the administration has no intention of yielding its authority over resource allocation to us. So unless we want to relinquish our responsibility for educational policy to them, we must insist that we and they work as co-equal partners in all phases of campus academic planning.

But we must do more than insist. We also must establish internal procedures that will make that kind of cooperation possible (*Record of the Assembly*, 1972, p. 4).

The environment for such cooperation is improving. Several institutions reported in words similar to those used by the University of Michigan: The campus has "a better environment to coordinate academic programs and to evaluate alternative uses of funds." Partly, of course, the new attitude sets a climate for change because it encourages planning, also an observation made by many of the institutions.

There are other kinds of evidence that a new climate, conducive to change, exists on campus. It is revealed by the way the colleges and universities handle that most sensitive issue—how to talk about their finances. The secrecy apparent in the first study is now, for the most part, gone. At that time, many administrators were very concerned lest the study report financial trouble at their institution. They didn't mind the implication that trouble might be on the way if an alert constituency did not help. But the implication that trouble was at hand was seen as an admission of defeat, incompetence, or both.

Today, in contrast, many institutions (including several that complained about the explicit reporting in *New Depression*) have prepared candid reports of their financial problems, reporting the trouble, and how the institution is planning to deal with it. In a bold move, New York University ran a full-page ad in *The New York Times* ("What New York University . . .," 1972, p. 15). Ohio University has introduced the most effective method of any uncovered by this study for making financial issues public. The university's internal budget hearings covering all financial decisions are broadcast on the campus (and community) radio station. The hearings are held in a campus auditorium and students, faculty, and townspeople are invited to attend and ask questions. Many do. This year's hearing ran for four days—a broadcast of 40 hours.

Where once financial trouble was feared as evidence of failure, today it is increasingly seen as an opportunity to demonstrate the capacity to change and cope.

Several colleges point out that financial stress also creates pressures against change. Some of these are the understandable reactions of persons threatened with layoff—union pressures against cost-saving measures and the natural inclination to dig in. While it is clear from campus reports that these counterpressures exist, as of now, they are clearly overcome by the pressures for change.

The managed institution   Finally, there is a fourth aspect to the new attitudes on campus emerging as a result of financial stringency—that is the acceptance of the idea of the managed university or college. To one not familiar with academic institutions, the declaration that the acceptance of the "managed institution" is a new attitude might at first seem strange. Are these expensive institutions not managed? To a large extent they have not been. In considerable measure that has been one of their great strengths. They have been decentralized, largely autonomous institutions, relying on shared values and assumptions for their coherence and their ability to operate, and relying on individuals' academic entrepreneurship for innovation and development. These values and assumptions worked well. Colleges and universities went through their period of remarkable growth despite the fact that they had been severely undermanaged. In some excellent institutions, budgets were weak tools, if they existed. The institutions made little effort to study themselves, and their members felt very little need to be managed.

In a recent speech, Sir Eric Ashby represented the concern of those who see that undermanaged world changing rapidly:

Cost-benefit analyses can be applied to vocational education; a vocational qualification probably puts up the earnings of the person who possesses it and possibly benefits the economy. But cost-benefit analysis applied to non-vocational education is a nonsense; indeed such education may be counter-productive, producing men and women who not only eschew high-income careers for themselves but even reject and oppose the commonly accepted norms of Western society such as the necessity for an ever-increasing GNP. Cost-benefit analysis can doubtless suggest ways in which mass higher education can be more efficiently conducted; but it would be positively inefficient to try to increase the efficiency of that sector devoted to minority "hand-made" education. We still can't teach or learn at this level any faster than our ancestors in medieval Oxford. An illuminating comment I heard recently in a discussion of the arts is equally applicable to this level of higher education: despite all our advances in technology it still takes 3 man-hours to play a 45-minute Schubert quartet. Technology enables more people to hear the quartet; but technology never will improve the productivity of the performers (Ashby, 1973, p. 00).

Significantly, the organization that sponsored Sir Eric's speech has also published an important volume with quite a different outlook: *Higher Education—From Autonomy to System* (1972). That new book reflects the times. Institutions are engaged in self-study, cost analyses, and experiments in simulation. They are working to learn what the institution now is, what it wants to be, and the most effective ways of getting there. And the institutions themselves are being grouped into large systems. All of this requires management.

The idea of the managed institution is now explored in rather searching papers (Millet, 1972), it is surveyed by conference reports (*Personnel management . . .*, 1972), it is talked about from a comparative vantage point (Besse, 1972), it has become the subject of a special Aspen Seminar (*The Contributions . . .*, 1972), is being worked at in Europe,[4] and, fortunately, has become the object of some humor (Pierson, 1973, p. 12).

NEW PRACTICES AND RELATIONSHIPS

Responses from administrators reveal that almost all of the campuses in the study are on the way to becoming managed institutions. Some have done a great deal to reach that state.

Although it may not always begin that way, the move toward becoming a managed university or college soon centers around the development of an overall strategy. The aim is an integrated planning process, one which is not overtaken by events but has the ability to respond to the times. The follow-up questionnaire asked administrators at each institution, "Have you adopted an overall strategy for dealing with your cost-income problems? Describe in detail." The responses (and their elaboration in two further questions) warrant the generalization that almost all are moving in this direction. Administrators at 30 institutions responded that they had adopted overall strategies, and described them in considerable detail (in several instances with supplementary materials that had been published for campus or public distribution). At five schools administrators said that what they had done could not yet be called a formal "overall strategy," but that they were working in that direction and knew that they had to do so. The remaining six institutions responded "no," they had not developed overall strategies. But even in these institutions, responses to other questions show that they have been doing selective cost cutting and taking various other measures, though apparently not yet in an integrated way. Of the six institutions in this group—those who have not sought to develop an overall strategy—two are private and four are public.

---

[4]In its Paris headquarters, the Office for Economic Cooperation and Development has a research unit devoted to the problems of management in higher education.

New attention to costs Colleges and universities have always paid attention to the task of raising income. The managed institution makes expenditure reduction an equal, or perhaps for a time, a first principle. Historically, the college president saw his job as maximizing inputs rather than maximizing outputs. The money inputs have generally been equated with quality. Thus the phrase "high-cost, high-quality" education is often used to describe a select group of undergraduate institutions. Students of educational finance have learned from Chancellor Howard R. Bowen of the Claremont University Center that it is income that determines expenditure, and that for most institutions income and expenditure are the same. The main factor determining the level of expenditure is the level of income. It is not surprising that the administrators who presided over the transformation of educational institutions from an elite to a mass stage would be oriented toward increasing income.

The new strategy still gives income an important place, to be sure. Many of the responses deal with fund raising, capital campaigns, and more sophisticated methods of handling endowment and its accounting.

But these tend to be swamped in detail, and, it seems fair to judge, in importance, by attention to reduction of expenditure. The important new fact is that reduction of expenditure growth is now as central, or more central, to administrative outlook than increasing income. One institution responded to the questionnaire by saying that "our major effort has always been seeking additional funds. Now we are required to work just as hard on cost reduction and avoidance." The phrase speaks for most of the schools in the study.

Cost cutting: what works? The questionnaire asked administrators "In your efforts to cut costs, what works? What doesn't work?" The long responses to both questions seem to indicate that administrators have had ample experience with both. The lists are revealing as much for what they say about the transition of academic organizations as for the specific items they include. Thus, from the "what doesn't work" category, there is general agreement that exhortation, appeals, talking and even "whining" do not work. It is agreed that appeals for voluntary efforts by operating units are not effective. "Don't expect the initiative to come from operating units," several answers say, "it must come from the central administration." That administration, say the respondents, must be adequately staffed but not overloaded. It must have capacity to take action. It cannot appear to act arbitrarily. In program reductions or in transfers, the administration must not show rigidity. It must make the effort to have those affected understand the context of the action taken. The most often-cited examples of arbitrariness that doesn't work is standardized, across-the-board cuts. Finally, although informed, directed cutting works, it works only to a point. Whether it is maintenance, salaries, positions, or libraries, many respondents warn, "Don't cut too far."

What works? The answers present an impressive array of actions that offer savings: Deferring, freezing, cutting, pooling various activities; better purchasing, more efficient scheduling, or improved food handling in dormitories. The schools are using a wide variety of devices that save money and are the kinds of things traditionally associated with good, inventive business management.

More important than these specific actions, however, are the organizational responses necessary to deal with the cost-income squeeze. Most answers to the questionnaire agree that first, there must be what several respondents call a better decision structure. "Better" is used to mean responsive, responsible, and one with power to set and control targets, one with more central authority. It is clear that an organizational imperative is power to set guidelines for performance by the units within the campus. There are various ways to do this. One campus reports that it asks each unit to submit a base budget at 97 percent and set priorities up to 110 percent. Another says it assigns costs to operating units, gives them guidelines and specific targets, and then helps them, through management analysis, to clarify their choices and move to their real objectives. Another says it uses central decision power to decentralize responsibility for operating successfully within specific terms—essentially the "every tub on its own bottom" principle.

All agree it is desirable to gain participation from the campus community—staff, faculty, students—so that its members are informed about decisions that will affect them, will know the seriousness of the need, and can develop the leadership orientation needed.

New administrative role What these responses reveal is that in the managed institution there is a changed role for the administration. In the managed institution, the administrators are the managers. Their function is changing in a way central to the operation of the institutions. Somewhat oversimplified, it can be said that in the recent past new programming was the product of opportunity, a result of faculty initiative. After a new program decision was made, the administrator's job was to take care of the necessary housekeeping and see to the details needed to make the programs operate. Now, it is the administrator's task to provide in advance the conditions that make operations and new programs possible. From his former role in making arrangements after decisions had been made, the administrator is now becoming the key element in deciding whether, when, and on what terms change is possible. As one institution responded, "opportunity programming has been replaced by forward programming geared to assured resources." In short, the administrator has gone from residual claimant to director.

Inevitably, this change raises the question of the role of faculty, students, and trade unionism. The faculty speech to the senate noted earlier was a recognition that this process, though not intended to be a substitute for academic planning nor to usurp the faculty's role in academic planning, can in fact unwittingly yield these results. It now takes special effort to insure participation in the process. Thus, we find many of the institutions establishing faculty-student committees, designed to assure participation in the planning and budgeting process. University of Michigan administrators responded in their questionnaire:

> The University has established three faculty-student committees to deal with the immediate and long run problems of budget priorities, program evaluation, and long range planning. These Committee will consider internal budget allocations for reassignment of funds if possible, will evaluate programs to determine whether they should be continued, reduced, enlarged, or otherwise changed, and will attempt to project for ten to twenty years long-run relationships of costs and income.

The model for this approach was the successful Committee on Priorities at Princeton. New York University, in financial trouble, found use of a task force very helpful in making sharp adjustments in its operations.

Thus the problem becomes one of cooperation and of maintaining creative tension between somewhat different constituencies at a time of changing roles for administrators.

The move toward becoming a managed campus is not a change from no management, but a change from one of gentle undermanagement. Most campuses have long been familiar with such activities as budgets, plans, and control devices, but these activities were more often than not seen as satisfying some remote bureaucratic requirement that probably provided employment to otherwise worthy people who were not essential to an academic mission. Today, the internal requirements of management are becoming central to the campus existence. Just three years ago planning was a fragmented activity at Rutgers University. Only one staff member (an associate provost) devoted full-time to the activity. Today that function is centralized, directed by a vice-president for program development and budgeting (who supervises directors of management analysis, university studies, and budget planning). The total staff is about 25 persons. This is a typical situation. In most institutions, planning was once remote from the line of decision and not related to budgeting. But no longer. Most institutions are adding strength to their administrative capacity and making it a visible part of the decision processes. This requires high quality administrators. Today, the college president must pay as much attention to who his business officer is as to who his dean of the college is.

Just a few years ago, the managers of higher education knew their place—it was at the periphery. Now the gravity of financial matters has drawn them to the center. It is around their calculations that increasingly other things must revolve.

6. Longer-run Stability: The Prospects and Its Implications

FINANCIAL
PROSPECTS The main finding from this look, two years later, at the 41 institutions is that most seem to have achieved a tentatively stabilized financial situation. That stability is fragile, for it is the product of unusual cuts in expenditure growth and is based in part on favorable assumptions about external conditions—inflation, enrollments, private support, and public policy at the state and federal levels. Clearly, then, it would not take much to destroy the stability and force the institutions on a downward course again. The most obvious question raised by this finding is: Will the stability last?

What if the external conditions are themselves stabilized? Is that enough to continue the stability of the institutions? Apparently not. The responses from the administrators indicate that for a general condition of stability to continue for the longer run, the present expenditure-income relationships will have to improve. Of the 41 institutions in the study, 23 indicate that their situation would be "about the same" if present trends continue, but 18 predict that their financial condition would deteriorate. In short, for almost half of the institutions, the present, somewhat favorable trends are not enough. Moreover, as we have said, the internal situation is based on too much deferral of costs.

We have no measure to indicate precisely what it would take to make the current stability a longer-run condition, but we do have some indications of what is involved. Most obviously, the colleges and universities cannot continue to operate at a level of expenditure growth as low as the most recent finding of 0.5 above the rate of inflation. Although they cannot realistically aspire to return to the "Golden Year" levels of expenditure growth, they must be able to have some expenditure growth. For these purposes, a figure that approximates the 2.5 recommended by the Carnegie Commission seems reasonable. At the time that recommendation was made, the Commission seemed to regard it as a bit harsh. But our findings indicate that during the last two years the institutions have been operating at an even lower expenditure level.

The rapidly growing management movement in higher education will create the capacity for institutions to operate with stability at lower levels of expenditure growth. Therefore, if income levels come up to a level approximating the Carnegie Commission recommendations of 2.5, it is reasonable to expect longer-term stability. Even this will leave some institutions in difficulty because of exceptional circumstances. It seems likely that these will be relatively few in number.

If this level of income support for higher education is not achieved, the crisis nature of the problem will reappear. Then, given the deep level of expenditure cuts, the postponed faculty salary adjustments, the deferred maintenance, the stakes will be very high.

Whether income levels will permit the institutions to grow at a modest but reliable level, such as the 2.5 percent figure, depends, as we have seen, on external factors. But these in turn very much depend upon what the institutions themselves do. If they are reasonably governable, reasonably efficient, and justify support in terms of an acceptable mission, we believe the historic conditions for adequate support will prevail. Thus, we need to analyze what the institutions are doing in terms that enable us to evaluate their prospects for support.

DECISION MAKING IN THE STABLE STATE The depression in higher education is new, and in some ways so is the nature of the response of colleges and universities. The original study concluded that the campuses were dealing not with the traditional money problem of the colleges, but with a new cost-income problem. Now, two years later, we have seen that what is happening on campus is not just a traditional business response to a money problem. The adjustment process has generated and reflects new managerial practices and organizational relationships. Although their immediate object is to make ends meet, they will inevitably work change in academic policy, converting questions of money into questions of purpose. As we noted at the outset, this process of institutionalizing new practices and relationships has developed faster in some institutions than in others. One cannot generalize about the situation in all institutions, but it is possible to characterize this evolving system and contrast it with the methods it is replacing.

1   *The stimulus for change is financial and internal.* Since World War II the main stimulus for change in higher education has been external. Demand for higher education expanded, and the schools had a wide variety of options to choose in shaping and serving others' needs. The recent history of higher education has been a record of responsive institutions growing or adding functions in the service of the larger society. There was the need to grow to accommodate new students; then the demand for science and language to accommodate national purpose; the request for research for the nation's defense needs; and

most recently, the urgent plea for social purpose in the cities. That is not the situation today. While these and similar pressures have not disappeared, they are small compared to the internal financial pressures. Today's colleges and universities are concerned primarily with defining and serving their own need to support operations.

2   *Internal financial pressure makes decisions increasingly interdependent.* In the recent period of growth, decisions about educational policy or about a new fringe benefit were typically seen as independent actions to be judged on their own merits. "When times were easier and money was more readily available, we each could proceed with our delegated responsibilities relatively independent of the other . . .," the faculty leader told the academic senate in the speech cited earlier (p. 63). "Now," the speech continues, "times no longer are easy and money no longer is readily available, and our two functions [faculty and administration] are no longer independent or even very separable." In the increasingly steady state, there are no independent decisions; priorities are always relative, and scarcity puts a premium on avoiding mistakes. Hence the growing popularity of simulation techniques that reveal the effect various types of decisions would have on the institution..

3   *The method of change is by substitution or even contraction, but not by growth.* All organizations like to change the easiest way, by growing. Until recently that has been the main method of change for colleges and universities. In contrast, today, with diminishing growth and an approaching steady-state condition, change cannot be by growth but must be by careful planning, by substitution, even by contraction. A steady-state condition and continuing financial stress put great emphasis on choice from among alternatives. A curriculum decision raises more than the question whether it is academically good to add a particular new field; in addition, it puts the choice of what other work would have to be abandoned. Desired change therefore depends on informed choice. Under the method of change by growth, faculty members instituted changes, and administrators did what was necessary to accommodate the change. Today, the administrators work comes first, gathering and analyzing information that will inform the choices that must be made if a change is to occur. Over time, change through informed choice forces a statement of values as well. To what extent these values will be the product of educational policy or of extra-academic forces is not yeat clear; we will refer to that issue shortly.

4   *To be credible, change by substitution or by contraction must be based on systems.* Integrity in decisions that depend upon choice requires systematic methods for making the choices. In order to establish informed, credible decisions about priorities, it is necessary to gather data on what is done, how much it costs, what the various benefits are. No

administrator can defend choices made under difficult circumstances unless they are supported by a decent empirical rationale together with careful consideration of qualitative elements. Therefore, institutions functioning under the above circumstances must develop systems— information systems, budget systems, and eventually systems for decision making. The old method relied on faculty entrepreneurship, the new one relies on comparable data needed for decision. One university president, in a recent comment on this point, noted that formerly if one of his departments wanted another secretary, the matter would be argued out, and a decision made. "Today, we would be guided not by arguments, but by a computer print-out that compared workloads in all departments."

5 *Systems require that decision points be focused and powers defined.* Decentralized, nonsystematic decision making tends to be a diffuse process, not very well defined. For academics, its great virtue has been that it was a process which could be influenced at several points; although it was not very tidy, it was open to academic influence. When the exercise of influence is easy, the formal allocation of power does not raise many questions. In contrast, systems require that decision points be focused, powers of the participants defined, and time deadlines established. No doubt one basis of the trend toward faculty unionization is the felt need for a device through which faculty can influence the more tidy process of systematic decision making.

6 *Criteria for judgment under planned change are measurable and institutionalized.* The old maxim "no academic experiment ever fails" is on the way out. The rationalization that every experiment produces some information and expresses some academic value is no longer considered defensible. Better points of reference are being developed, for systems-guided decisions ideally require measuring the desired result. These may not become rigorous, but they will effectively challenge the standards often used by department-oriented faculty members, such as the approval of colleagues elsewhere, and will but more emphasis on local campus needs. When resources are scarce, the planning and decision process must include a statement of the results desired. There will be an increasing effort to measure the outputs, or the outcomes (as they are sometimes called), of higher education. As these become the basis for decision making, there will be a relative decline in the influence of individual academic value preferences of faculty members. Thus will questions of money be converted to questions of academic purpose.

IMPLICATIONS FOR QUALITY AND PURPOSE To a large extent, the foregoing characteristics of the evolving system of university decision making are the result of scarcity. But, in another sense, they exemplify trends that have probably existed throughout the postwar period—namely, the tendency of higher education to respond to the needs of the outside community and consequently to accept outside value judgments in the making of educational policy. Certainly, the dynamics of the schools' reaction to scarcity illustrates the interplay of outside pressures, academic values, and even rather specific academic policies. We have suggested that the new practices and organizational relationships of the schools have influenced standards of judgment about educational quality and purpose. Consider some concepts now being modified or abandoned as revealed or suggested by the responses to the questionnaire in this relatively small study:

1 *Size*   The assumed importance of small classes to superior instruction is giving way to the need to increase income. So, too, is the low student-faculty ratio. Most institutions are increasing both. Even the idea that small campuses are better than larger ones is giving way to the need to increase income. Some small institutions have plans for limited growth.

2 *Richness of mixture*   In spite of the view that the richer the mixture of offerings the better, courses, programs, and even parts of campuses are now being dropped. The idea that more, or longer, is better is giving way to proposals for reducing the time for various degrees. Academic judgment about the best campus mix is beginning to give way to market judgments. If a major unit of the campus does not pay its way, its future is precarious.

3 *Environment for learning and teaching*   The assumption that the campus is an essential part of the learning environment is now challenged by the off-campus models, which are claimed to be as good, and cheaper. The assumption that academic excellence required freedom based on assuring faculty members of secure employment is now giving way to layoffs of faculty members, and even experiments to modify the tenure system.

4 *Value of education itself*   The measurable result has created doubt about the idea that there is an objective, social importance in promoting whatever may be the inherent values of education. The more fashionable view just now is that the public benefits of education are not very high or very clear and that education is an activity that mainly produces private benefits.

If this list is at all representative, the conversion of questions of money to questions of purpose has been mainly one of challenging existing ideas about education. To a considerable extent this must be regarded as healthy. Along with the expenditure cuts, these challenges will, in time, produce convincing evidence that the campuses are reasonably efficient in their internal operations. As we noted in Chapter 2, such evidence of efficiency seems to be a condition for increased public contribution to the income of higher education. Moreover, there is no strong reason to conclude that these challenges to old assumptions about quality in education have seriously reduced quality. The follow-up questionnaire did not ask administrators to evaluate quality. Some discussed it, and from these and from conversations with administrators, it would seem that most would say that quality of their institutions has not declined very much, despite the kinds of modifications noted. Standards are not the same as two years ago. And perhaps, on any standards, some of the old assumptions were unsound.

It is one thing to say that the challenge to existing dogma may be healthy. It is quite another thing to find in the current situation the genesis of an affirmative sense of purpose in higher education that might assure continued financial stability. Two of the three conditions we suggested in *New Depression*—and, again, in Chapter 2 of this study—for the increased investment in higher education necessary to assure its long-run stability seem attainable. The campuses seem reasonably governable. This follow-up study indicates that most institutions should be able to demonstrate in the future reasonable efficiency in internal operations. The demonstration of a comprehensible and persuasive set of unifying purposes remains.

Is higher education likely to develop a sustaining and unifying set of purposes in the predictable future? Our analysis in this chapter suggests that the process of dealing with the new depression is generating a system of procedural values. This trend is likely to be reinforced by public policy. As Chapter 2 indicates, the federal approach to higher education now seems committed to the use of market techniques. As these developments create further challenges to existing ideas about education, their limitations will also become clearer. Systems for decision making do not tell one what are the best objectives in educational terms. An educational market place does not come preequiped with consumer protection, adequate information, prices that permit free choice, or safeguards from government interference.[1]

Systems are meaningful only in the context of their environment. The present environment, off campus and on, is conducive to objectives defined in terms of efficiency and competitve response to market demand. The development of coherent educational options for the consumer will take much more effort. Yet in the long run, this effort will be most rewarding. It is not unfair to believe that the new depression

---

[1] For an excellent analysis of the misconceptions in the currently fashionable "manpower" approach to educational policy, see Bowen (1973, pp. 5-14).

was in considerable part shaped by growth more responsive to market considerations than to educational values. Now under financial pressure, academic institutions have a unique if difficult opportunity to assert educational values. Forced to redefine their mission, they can responsibly help determine their future.

References

American Association of University Professors: *Depression: Recovery and Higher Education*, McGraw-Hill Book Company, New York, 1937.

American Council on Education: *New Academic Institutions*, Washington, D.C., 1972.

"Annual Report for 1971-72," Council for Financial Aid to Education, New York, 1972.

Ashby, Eric: *The Structure of Higher Education: A World View*, International Council for Educational Development, New York, Occasional Paper No. 6, January 1973.

Besse, Ralph: "A Comparison of the University with the Corporation," *AGB Reports*, vol. 15, no. 3, pp. 2-14, Nov.-Dec., 1972.

Bowen, Howard R.: "Manpower Management and Higher Education," *Educational Record*, vol. 54, pp. 5-14, Winter 1973.

Carnegie Commission on Higher Education: *More Effective Use of Resources: An Imperative for Higher Education*, McGraw-Hill Book Company, New York, 1972.

Cheit, Earl: *The New Depression in Higher Education*, McGraw-Hill Book Company, New York, February 1971.

Chronicle of Higher Education, vol. 6, no. 20, p. 4, Feb. 22, 1972.

Chronicle of Higher Education, vol. 7, no. 5, pp. 1 and 2, Oct. 24, 1972.

The Contributions of Business Management to Higher Education Management, Academy for Educational Development, Washington, D.C., November 1972.

Higher Education—From Autonomy to System, International Council for Educational Development, New York, 1972.

Jellema, William: *The Financial Conditions of Higher Education—and the Expenditures that Brought Them To It*, prepared for Council on Educational Development, Task Force on Alternate Sources of College Funding, unpublished.

Jellema, William W.: *The Red and the Black–Special Preliminary Report on the Financial Status, Present and Projected, of Private Institutions of Higher Learning*, Association of American Colleges, Washington, D.C., 1971.

Jenny, Hans H., and G. Richard Wynn: *The Golden Years*, College of Wooster, Wooster, Ohio, 1970.

Kerr, Clark: "Presidential Discontent," in David C. Nichols (ed.), *Perspectives on Campus Tensions: Papers Prepared for the Special Committee on Campus Tensions*, American Council on Education, Washington, D.C., September 1970.

Millett, John D.: "The Crisis in Higher Education Management," presented at Conference on Management by Objectives in Higher Education, Washington, D.C., Nov. 9, 1972, unpublished.

O'Neill, June: *Resource Use in Higher Education*, Carnegie Commission on Higher Education, Berkeley, Calif., 1971.

Ottina, John: "1202 Commissions Put Off Indefinitely, Ottina Announces," *Higher Education and National Affairs*, vol. 22, no. 10, p. 1, March 9, 1973.

Personnel Management in Higher Education, Academy for Educational; Development, Washington, D.C., 1972.

Pierson, George A.: "Competing for Power in Today's University," *Chronicle on Higher Education*, vol. 7, no. 17, p. 12, Jan. 29, 1973.

Record of the Assembly, University of California Academic Senate, vol. 10, no. 1, p. 4, Nov. 29, 1972.

Steiner, Peter O., Maryse Eymonerie, and William B. Woolf: "Coping with Adversity: Report on the Economic Status of the Profession, 1971-1972," *AAUP Bulletin*, vol. 58, no. 2, pp. 178-195, June 1972.

Trends in State Funding in Higher Education: A Preliminary Report, Education Commission of the States, Report 33, Denver, 1973.

"What New York University Can Be, and What it Cannot Be," *New York Times*, p. 15, May 30, 1972.

Appendix

Institution

This questionnaire is part of a follow-up study of *The New Depression in Higher Education*. We are sending this questionnaire to each of the 41 colleges and universities in the original study. We appreciate your cooperation. Please return the completed form to: Earl F. Cheit, 350 Barrows Hall, Univeristy of California, Berkeley, California, 94720.

1. How would you characterize the present financial condition of your institution?

2. If present cost and income trends were to continue for the next three years, what would be the main effects on your institution?

3. How does the current financial condition compare with that of two years ago (June 1970)?

    (a) In what ways is it better?

    (b) In what ways is it worse?

4. To what extent and in what ways is the difference between your present situation and that of June 1970 due to external influences?

    internal influences?

5. Has your institution adopted an overall strategy for dealing with cost-income problems? _____

Please indicate its main elements (both cost and income):

_____
_____
_____
_____

6. Have you found that modern management techniques for planning and decision making are helpful in solving your cost-income problems? _____

_____
_____
_____

7. In your efforts to cut costs, what works? _____

_____
_____
_____

What doesn't work? _____

_____
_____

8. In a recent report, the Carnegie Commission estimates that through more effective use of resources individual institutions could cut one percentage point from their average annual (1960's rate of) increase in expenditures per student, and in addition that an equivalent sum could be cut from the increasing total cost of higher education if institutions accelerated and integrated academic programs. Does your experience lead you to agree with these two conclusions? _____

_____
_____
_____

9. Has the funding pattern for your institution changed significantly in the last two years? _____

_____
_____

10. According to your best dollar estimates for the coming academic year, how much would your institution benefit from the Higher

Education Act of 1972 if the Act were fully funded by Congress?

_____

What is your prediction of the actual dollar benefits to your institution?_____

Do you expect the Act to have a significant impact on your financial situation in the future?_____

Please note any other comments on the Higher Education Act of 1972 or on legislative approaches you recommend _____

_____

_____

_____

11. In what ways, if any, has financial stringency had beneficial impacts on your institution?_____

_____

_____

12. Is your faculty organized in a collective bargaining unit?
    If not, is collective bargaining with your faculty a likely prospect in the next three years? _____

13. Do you have any other comments on the financial condition and prospects for your institution? _____

_____

14. Excluding your own institution, would you be willing to list one (or more) institution(s) comparable to your own (e.g., state college, research university, community college, liberal arts college) which you believe to be very well managed?_____

_____

15. Could you please furnish us with the following:
    (1) current operating expenses (excluding sponsored research, student aid, and auxiliary enterprises) for the academic years
        1969/70 $_____ 1970/71 $_____
        1971/72 $_____ 1972/73 (if available) $____
    (2) enrollment figures (using the same basis each year, head count or full-time equivalent)
        Fall of 1969 _____ 1971_____
            1970_____ 1972 if available_____

The paragraph below was excerpted from the notes of the interviewer who visited your campus in 1970. It appears in *The New Depression in Higher Education* as a brief statement of what the financial problem looked like to the campus at that time. We would very much appreciate your sending us a statement of comparable length that conveys the sense of your current financial situation from your perspective. Please use the next page for your statement.

Carnegie Commission on Higher Education
Sponsored Research Studies

THE UNIVERSITY AS AN ORGANIZATION
James S. Perkins (ed.)

WHERE COLLEGES ARE AND
WHO ATTENDS:
EFFECTS OF ACCESSIBILITY ON
COLLEGE ATTENDANCE
*C. Arnold Anderson, Mary Jean
Bowman and Vincent Tinto*

THE EMERGING TECHNOLOGY:
INSTRUCTIONAL USE OF THE
COMPUTER IN HIGHER
EDUCATION
Roger E. Levien

NEW DIRECTIONS IN LEGAL
EDUCATION
Herbert L. Packer and Thomas Ehrlich

A STATISTICAL PORTRAIT OF
HIGHER EDUCATION
Seymour E. Harris

EDUCATION AND EVANGELISM:
A PROFILE OF PROTESTANT COLLEGES
C. Robert Pace

THE HOME OF SCIENCE:
THE ROLE OF THE UNIVERSITY
Dael Wolfle

PROFESSIONAL EDUCATION:
SOME NEW DIRECTIONS
Edgar H. Schein

THE NONPROFIT RESEARCH
INSTITUTE: ITS ORIGIN, OPERATION,
PROBLEMS, AND PROSPECTS
Harold Orlans

THE INVISIBLE COLLEGES:
A PROFILE OF SMALL, PRIVATE
COLLEGES WITH LIMITED RESOURCES
Alexander W. Astin and Calvin B. T. Lee

AMERICAN HIGHER EDUCATION:
DIRECTIONS OLD AND NEW
Joseph Ben-David

A DEGREE AND WHAT ELSE?:
CORRELATES AND CONSEQUENCES OF
A COLLEGE EDUCATION
*Stephen B. Withey, Jo Anne Coble, Gerald
Gurin, John P. Robinson, Burkhard Strumpel,
Elizabeth Keogh Taylor, and Arthur C. Wolfe*

THE MULTICAMPUS UNIVERSITY:
A STUDY OF ACADEMIC GOVERNANCE
Eugene C. Lee and Frank M. Bowen

INSTITUTIONS IN TRANSITION:
A PROFILE OF CHANGE IN HIGHER
EDUCATION
(INCORPORATING THE 1970
STATISTICAL REPORT)
Harold L. Hodgkinson

EFFICIENCY IN LIBERAL EDUCATION:
A STUDY OF COMPARATIVE INSTRUC-
TIONAL COSTS FOR DIFFERENT WAYS
OF ORGANIZING TEACHING-LEARNING
IN A LIBERAL ARTS COLLEGE
Howard R. Bowen and Gordon K. Douglass

CREDIT FOR COLLEGE:
PUBLIC POLICY FOR STUDENT LOANS
Robert W. Hartman

MODELS AND MAVERICKS:
A PROFILE OF PRIVATE LIBERAL
ARTS COLLEGES
Morris T. Keeton

BETWEEN TWO WORLDS:
A PROFILE OF NEGRO HIGHER
EDUCATION
Frank Bowles and Frank A. DeCosta

BREAKING THE ACCESS BARRIERS:
A PROFILE OF TWO-YEAR COLLEGES
Leland L. Medsker and Dale Tillery

ANY PERSON, ANY STUDY:
AN ESSAY ON HIGHER EDUCATION IN
THE UNITED STATES
Eric Ashby

THE NEW DEPRESSION IN HIGHER
EDUCATION:
A STUDY OF FINANCIAL CONDITIONS
AT 41 COLLEGES AND UNIVERSITIES
Earl F. Cheit

FINANCING MEDICAL EDUCATION:
AN ANALYSIS OF ALTERNATIVE
POLICIES AND MECHANISMS
Rashi Fein and Gerald I. Weber

HIGHER EDUCATION IN NINE
COUNTRIES:
A COMPARATIVE STUDY OF COLLEGES
AND UNIVERSITIES ABROAD
*Barbara B. Burn, Philip G. Altbach, Clark
Kerr, and James A. Perkins*

BRIDGES TO UNDERSTANDING:
INTERNATIONAL PROGRAMS OF AMER-
ICAN COLLEGES AND UNIVERSITIES
Irwin T. Sanders and Jennifer C. Ward

GRADUATE AND PROFESSIONAL
EDUCATION, 1980:
A SURVEY OF INSTITUTIONAL PLANS
Lewis B. Mayhew

THE AMERICAN COLLEGE AND
AMERICAN CULTURE:
SOCIALIZATION AS A FUNCTION OF
HIGHER EDUCATION
Oscar and Mary F. Handlin

RECENT ALUMNI AND HIGHER
EDUCATION:
A SURVEY OF COLLEGE GRADUATES
Joe L. Spaeth and Andrew M. Greeley

CHANGE IN EDUCATIONAL POLICY:
SELF-STUDIES IN SELECTED COLLEGES
AND UNIVERSITIES
Dwight R. Ladd

STATE OFFICIALS AND HIGHER
EDUCATION:
A SURVEY OF THE OPINIONS AND
EXPECTATIONS OF POLICY MAKERS IN
NINE STATES
Heinz Eulau and Harold Quinley

ACADEMIC DEGREE STRUCTURES:
INNOVATIVE APPROACHES
PRINCIPLES OF REFORM IN DEGREE
STRUCTURES IN THE UNITED STATES
Stephen H. Spurr

COLLEGES OF THE FORGOTTEN
AMERICANS:
A PROFILE OF STATE COLLEGES
AND REGIONAL UNIVERSITIES
E. Alden Dunham

FROM BACKWATER TO MAINSTREAM:
A PROFILE OF CATHOLIC HIGHER
EDUCATION
Andrew M. Greeley

THE ECONOMICS OF THE MAJOR
PRIVATE UNIVERSITIES
William G. Bowen
*(Out of print, but available from University
Microfilms.)*

THE FINANCE OF HIGHER EDUCATION
Howard R. Bowen
*(Out of print, but available from University
Microfilms.)*

ALTERNATIVE METHODS OF FEDERAL
FUNDING FOR HIGHER EDUCATION
Ron Wolk
*(Out of print, but available from University
Microfilms.)*

INVENTORY OF CURRENT RESEARCH
ON HIGHER EDUCATION 1968
Dale M. Heckman and Warren Bryan Martin
*(Out of print, but available from University
Microfilms.)*

*The following technical reports are available from the Carnegie Commission on
Higher Education, 1947 Center Street, Berkeley, California 94704.*

SOURCES OF FUNDS TO COLLEGES
AND UNIVERSITIES
June O'Neill

ESTIMATING THE RETURNS TO
EDUCATION: A DISAGGREGATED
APPROACH
Richard S. Eckaus

AN INVENTORY OF ACADEMIC
INNOVATION AND REFORM
Ann Heiss

PAPERS ON EFFICIENCY IN THE
MANAGEMENT OF HIGHER EDUCATION
*Alexander M. Mood, Colin Bell,
Lawrence Bogard, Helen Brownlee,
and Joseph McCloskey*

AMERICAN COLLEGE AND
UNIVERSITY ENROLLMENT
TRENDS IN 1971
Richard E. Peterson

MAY 1970:
THE CAMPUS AFTERMATH OF
CAMBODIA AND KENT STATE
Richard E. Peterson and John A. Bilorusky

TRENDS AND PROJECTIONS OF PHYSI-
CIANS IN THE UNITED STATES 1967-2002
Mark S. Blumberg

RESOURCE USE IN HIGHER EDUCATION:
TRENDS IN OUTPUT AND INPUTS,
1930-1967
June O'Neill

MENTAL ABILITY AND HIGHER
EDUCATIONAL ATTAINMENT IN THE
20TH CENTURY
Paul Taubman and Terence Wales

*The following reprints are available from the Carnegie Commission on Higher
Education, 1947 Center Street, Berkeley, California 94704.
(First copies of reprints are sent free on request. Enclose 20 cents each for
additional copies to defray costs of postage and handling.)*

MORE FOR LESS: HIGHER EDUCATION'S NEW PRIORITY, *by Virginia B. Smith,
reprinted from* UNIVERSAL HIGHER EDUCATION: COSTS AND BENEFITS, *American
Council on Education, Washington, D.C., 1971.*

ACADEMIA AND POLITICS IN AMERICA, *by Seymour M. Lipset, reprinted from Thomas
J. Nossiter (ed.),* IMAGINATION AND PRECISION IN THE SOCIAL SCIENCES, *pp.
211-289, Faber and Faber, London, 1972.*

POLITICS OF ACADEMIC NATURAL SCIENTISTS AND ENGINEERS, *by Everett C.
Ladd, Jr., and Seymour M. Lipset, reprinted from* SCIENCE, *vol. 176, no. 4039, pp. 1091-
1100, June 9, 1972.*

THE INTELLECTUAL AS CRITIC AND REBEL: WITH SPECIAL REFERENCE TO THE
UNITED STATES AND THE SOVIET UNION, *by Seymour M. Lipset and Richard B.
Dobson, reprinted from* DAEDALUS, *vol. 101, no. 3, pp. 137-198, Summer 1972.*

POLITICS OF AMERICAN SOCIOLOGISTS, *by Seymour M. Lipset and Everett C. Ladd,
Jr., reprinted from* AMERICAN JOURNAL OF SOCIOLOGY, *vol. 78, no. 1, pp. 67-104,
July 1972.*

THE DISTRIBUTION OF ACADEMIC TENURE IN AMERICAN HIGHER EDUCATION,
by Martin Trow, reprinted from Bardwell Smith (ed.), THE TENURE DEBATE, *Jossey-Bass,
San Francisco, 1972.*

THE NATURE AND ORIGINS OF THE CARNEGIE COMMISSION ON HIGHER EDUCATION,
*by Alan Pifer, based on a speech delivered to the Pennsylvania Association of Colleges and
Universities, Oct. 16, 1972, reprinted by permission of The Carnegie Foundation for the
Advancement of Teaching.*

FACULTY UNIONISM: FROM THEORY TO PRACTICE, *by Joseph W. Garbarino, reprinted from* INDUSTRIAL RELATIONS, *vol. 11, no. 1, pp. 1-17, February 1972.*

INTERNATIONAL PROGRAMS OF U.S. COLLEGES AND UNIVERSITIES: PRIORITIES FOR THE SEVENTIES, *by James A. Perkins, Occasional Paper No. 1, July 1971, reprinted by permission of the International Council for Educational Development.*

ACCELERATED PROGRAMS OF MEDICAL EDUCATION, *by Mark S. Blumberg, reprinted from* JOURNAL OF MEDICAL EDUCATION, *vol. 46, no. 8, August 1971.* *

SCIENTIFIC MANPOWER FOR 1970-1985, *by Allan M. Cartter, reprinted from* SCIENCE, *vol. 172, no. 3979, pp. 132-140, April 9, 1971.*

A NEW METHOD OF MEASURING STATES' HIGHER EDUCATION BURDEN, *by Neil Timm, reprinted from* THE JOURNAL OF HIGHER EDUCATION, *vol. 42, no. 1, pp. 27-33, January 1971.* *

REGENT WATCHING, *by Earl F. Cheit, reprinted from* AGB REPORTS, *vol. 13, no. 6, pp. 4-13, March 1971.* *

COLLEGE GENERATIONS–FROM THE 1930's TO THE 1960's, *by Seymour M. Lipset and Everett C. Ladd, Jr., reprinted from* THE PUBLIC INTEREST, *no. 24, Summer 1971.*

AMERICAN SOCIAL SCIENTISTS AND THE GROWTH OF CAMPUS POLITICAL ACTIVISM IN THE 1960s, *by Everett C. Ladd, Jr., and Seymour M. Lipset, reprinted from* SOCIAL SCIENCES INFORMATION, *vol. 10, no. 2, April 1971.*

THE POLITICS OF AMERICAN POLITICAL SCIENTISTS, *by Everett C. Ladd, Jr., and Seymour M. Lipset, reprinted from* PS, *vol. 4, no. 2, Spring 1971.* *

THE DIVIDED PROFESSORIATE, *by Seymour M. Lipset and Everett C. Ladd, Jr., reprinted from* CHANGE, *vol. 3, no. 3, pp. 54-60, May 1971.* *

JEWISH ACADEMICS IN THE UNITED STATES: THEIR ACHIEVEMENTS, CULTURE AND POLITICS, *by Seymour M. Lipset and Everett C. Ladd, Jr., reprinted from* AMERICAN JEWISH YEAR BOOK, *1971.*

THE UNHOLY ALLIANCE AGAINST THE CAMPUS, *by Kenneth Keniston and Michael Lerner, reprinted from* NEW YORK TIMES MAGAZINE, *November 8, 1970.*

PRECARIOUS PROFESSORS: NEW PATTERNS OF REPRESENTATION, *by Joseph W. Garbarino, reprinted from* INDUSTRIAL RELATIONS, *vol. 10, no. 1, February 1971.* *

. . . AND WHAT PROFESSORS THINK: ABOUT STUDENT PROTEST AND MANNERS, MORALS, POLITICS, AND CHAOS ON THE CAMPUS, *by Seymour Martin Lipset and Everett Carll Ladd, Jr., reprinted from* PSYCHOLOGY TODAY, *November 1970.* *

DEMAND AND SUPPLY IN U.S. HIGHER EDUCATION: A PROGRESS REPORT, *by Roy Radner and Leonard S. Miller, reprinted from* AMERICAN ECONOMIC REVIEW, *May 1970.* *

RESOURCES FOR HIGHER EDUCATION: AN ECONOMIST'S VIEW, *by Theodore W. Schultz, reprinted from* JOURNAL OF POLITICAL ECONOMY, *vol. 76, no. 3, University of Chicago, May/June 1968.* *

INDUSTRIAL RELATIONS AND UNIVERSITY RELATIONS, *by Clark Kerr, reprinted from* PROCEEDINGS OF THE 21ST ANNUAL WINTER MEETING OF THE INDUSTRIAL RELATIONS RESEARCH ASSOCIATION, *pp. 15-25.* *

NEW CHALLENGES TO THE COLLEGE AND UNIVERSITY, *by Clark Kerr, reprinted from Kermit Gordon (ed.),* AGENDA FOR THE NATION, *The Brookings Institution, Washington, D.C., 1968.* *

PRESIDENTIAL DISCONTENT, *by Clark Kerr, reprinted from David C. Nichols (ed.),* PERSPECTIVES ON CAMPUS TENSIONS: PAPERS PREPARED FOR THE SPECIAL COMMITTEE ON CAMPUS TENSIONS, *American Council on Education, Washington, D.C., September 1970.* *

STUDENT PROTEST—AN INSTITUTIONAL AND NATIONAL PROFILE, *by Harold Hodgkinson, reprinted from* THE RECORD, *vol. 71, no. 4, May 1970.* *

WHAT'S BUGGING THE STUDENTS?, *by Kenneth Keniston, reprinted from* EDUCATIONAL RECORD, *American Council on Education, Washington, D.C., Spring 1970.* *

THE POLITICS OF ACADEMIA, *by Seymour Martin Lipset, reprinted from David C. Nichols (ed.),* PERSPECTIVES ON CAMPUS TENSIONS: PAPERS PREPARED FOR THE SPECIAL COMMITTEE ON CAMPUS TENSIONS, *American Council on Education, Washington, D.C., September 1970.* *

COMING OF MIDDLE AGE IN HIGHER EDUCATION, *by Earl F. Cheit, reprinted by permission of National Association of State Universities and Land-Grant Colleges, Washington, D.C.*

*The Commission's stock of this reprint has been exhausted.